THE BEHAVIOR OF CROWDS

The
BEHAVIOR OF CROWDS
A Psychological Study

by
Everett Dean Martin

*Lecturer in Social Philosophy and Director of the Cooper
Union Forum of the People's Institute of New York*

HARPER & BROTHERS PUBLISHERS
NEW YORK AND LONDON

CONTENTS

FOREWORD

SINCE the publication of Le Bon's book, *The Crowd*, little has been added to our knowledge of the mechanisms of crowd-behavior. As a practical problem, the habit of crowd-making is daily becoming a more serious menace to civilization. Events are making it more and more clear that, pressing as are certain economic questions, the forces which threaten society are really psychological.

Interest in the economic struggle has to a large extent diverted attention from the significance of the problems of social psychology. Social psychology is still a rather embryonic science, and this notwithstanding the fact that psychiatry has recently provided us with a method with which we may penetrate more deeply than ever before into the inner sources of motive and conduct.

The remedy which I have suggested in Chapter X deserves a much more extended treatment than I have given it. It involves one of the great mooted questions of modern philosophical discussion. It is, however, not within the province of this book to enter upon a discussion of the philosophy of Humanism. The subject has been thoroughly thrashed over in philosophical journals and in the writings of James, Schiller, Dewey, and others. It is sufficient for my purpose merely to point out the fact that the humanist way of thinking may provide us with just that educational method which will break up the logical forms in which the crowd-mind intrenches itself.

Those who expect to find a prescribed formula or ideal scheme of organization as a remedy for our social ills may feel that the solution to which I have come—namely, a new educational method—is too vague. But the problem of the crowd is really concerned with the things of the mind. And if I am correct in my thesis that there is a necessary connection between crowd-thinking and the various traditional systems of intellectualist, absolutist, and rationalist philosophy, the way out must be through the formation of some such habits of thinking as I have suggested.

E. D. M.

New York, *October 10, 1919.*

THE BEHAVIOR OF CROWDS

I

THE CROWD AND THE SOCIAL PROBLEM OF TO-DAY

EVERY one at times feels himself in the grip of social forces over which he has no control. The apparently impersonal nature of these forces has given rise to various mechanistic theories of social behavior. There are those who interpret the events of history as by-products of economic evolution. Others, more idealistic but determinists, nevertheless, see in the record of human events the working out of a preordained plan.

There is a popular notion, often shared by scholars, that the individual and society are essentially irreconcilable principles. The individual is assumed to be by nature an anti-social being. Society, on the other hand, is opposed in principle to all that is personal and private. The demands of society, its welfare and aims, are treated as if they were a tax imposed upon each and every one by something foreign to the natural will or even the happiness of all. It is as if society as "thing-in-itself" could prosper in opposition to the individuals who collectively constitute it.

It is needless to say that both the individual and the social, according to such a view, are empty abstractions. The individual is, in fact, a social entity. Strip him of his social interests, endowments, and habits, and the very feeling of self, or "social me" as William James called it, vanishes and nothing is left but a Platonic idea and a reflex arc. The social also is nothing else than the manner in which individuals habitually react to one another. Society in the abstract, as a principle opposed to individual existence, has no more reality than that of the grin which Alice in Wonderland sees after the famous Cheshire cat has vanished. It is the mere logical concept of others in general, left leering at us after all the concrete others have been thought away.

Much social thinking is of this cat-grin sort. Having abstracted from the thought of self everything that is social, and from the idea of the social all that has to do with concrete persons, the task remains to get pure grin and pure cat together again in such a way that neither shall lose its identity in the other. It is, of course, impossible to reconcile these mutually exclusive abstractions either in theory or in practice. It is often difficult enough, even with the aid of empirical thinking, to adjust our relations with the other people about us. But on the Cheshire-cat hypothesis, the social problem can never be solved, because it is not a real problem at all.

Since the individual is therefore a social being as such, and the social is just a way of acting together, the social problem does not grow out of a conflict between the self and an impersonal social principle. The conflicts are, in fact, clashes among certain individuals and groups of them, or else—and this is a subject to which social psychology has paid insufficient attention—the social struggle is in certain of its phases a conflict within the personal psyche itself. Suppose that the apparently impersonal element in social behavior is not impersonal in fact, but is, for the most part, the result of an impersonal manner of thinking about ourselves. Every psychic fact must really be an act of somebody. There are no ideas without thinkers to think them, no impersonal thoughts or disembodied impulses, no "independent" truths, no transcendental principles existing in themselves and outside of human heads. Life is everywhere reaction; it is nowhere a mere product or a passive registering of impersonal forces. It is the organism's behavior in the presence of what we call environment.

Individual opinions cannot be tossed into a common hat, like small coins. Though we may each learn from the others, there is no magic by which our several thoughts can sum themselves up into a common fund of public opinion or super-personal whole which thinks itself, there being no collective head to think it. No matter how many people think and behave as I do, each of us knows only his own thought and behavior. My thought may be about you and what I judge you are thinking, but it is not the same as your thought. To each the social is *nil* except in so far as he experiences it himself, and to each it is something unique when viewed from within. The uniformity and illusion of identity—in short, the impersonal aspect of social thinking and activity appears only when we try to view social behavior from without—that is, as objectively manifest in the behavior of others.

What then is the secret of this impersonal view of the social? Why do we think of ourselves socially in the same impersonal or external way that we think of others? There is an interesting parallel here in the behavior of certain types of mental pathology. There are neurotics who commonly feel that certain aspects of their behavior are really not of their own authorship, but come to them as the

4

result of influences acting from without. It was such phenomena in part that led psychologists of a generation ago to construct the theory of "multiple personality." It is known now that the psychic material which in these cases appears to be automatic, and impersonal, in the sense that it is not consciously willed, is really motivated by unconscious mechanisms. The apparently "impersonal" behavior of the neurotic is psychologically determined, though unconsciously.

May there not be a like unconscious psychic determination of much that is called social behavior? It is my thesis that this is so, and that there are certain types of social behavior which are characterized by unconscious motivation to such a degree that they may be placed in a definite class of psychological phenomena. This group of phenomena I have, following to some extent the terminology of Le Bon, called "The Crowd." I wish there were a more exact word, for it is very difficult to use the word crowd in its psychological sense without causing some confusion in the mind of the reader. In ordinary speech "a crowd" is any gathering of people. In the writings of Le Bon, as we shall see, the word has a special meaning, denoting not a gathering of people as such, but a gathering which behaves in a certain way which may be classified and described psychologically as "crowd mentality,"

Not every gathering of people shows this crowd-mentality. It is a characteristic which appears under certain circumstances. In this discussion the word "crowd" must be understood to mean the peculiar mental condition which sometimes occurs when people think and act together, either immediately where the members of the group are present and in close contact, or remotely, as when they affect one another in a certain way through the medium of an organization, a party or sect, the press, etc.

The crowd while it is a social phenomenon differs greatly from the social as such. People may be social—the family is an example of this—without being a crowd either in thought or action. Again a crowd—a mob is an example of this—may be distinctly antisocial, if we attach any ethical meaning to the term. Both the individual and society suffer, as we shall see, from crowd-behavior. I know of nothing which to-day so menaces not only the values of civilization, but also—it is the same thing in other words, perhaps—the achievement of personality and true knowledge of self, as the growing habit of behaving as crowds.

Our society is becoming a veritable babel of gibbering crowds. Not only are mob outbreaks and riots increasing in number, but every interest, patriotic, religious, ethical,

6

political, economic, easily degenerates into a
confusion of propagandist tongues, into extravagant partisanship, and intemperance.
Whatever be the ideal to which we would
attain, we find the path of self-culture too
slow; we must become army worms, eating our
way to the goal by sheer force of numbers.
The councils of democracy are conducted on
about the psychological level of commercial
advertising and with about the same degree of
sincerity. While it cannot be said that the
habit of crowd-making is peculiar to our
times—other ages, too, have indulged in it—it
does seem that the tendency to crowd-
mindedness has greatly increased in recent
years.

Whether it is temperance, or justice, or
greater freedom, moral excellence or national
glory, that we desire—whether we happen to
be conservatives or radicals, reformers or
liberals, we must become a cult, write our
philosophy of life in flaming headlines, and
sell our cause in the market. No matter if
we meanwhile surrender every value for which
we stand, we must strive to cajole the majority
into imagining itself on our side. For only
with the majority with us, whoever we are,
can we live. It is numbers, not values,
that count — quantity not quality. Everybody must "moral-crusade," "agitate," "press-
agent," play politics. Everyone is forced to

speak as the crowd, think as the crowd, understand as the crowd. The tendency is to smother all that is unique, rare, delicate, secret. If you are to get anywhere in this progressive age you must be vulgar, you must add to your vulgarity unction. You must take sides upon dilemmas which are but half true, change the tempo of your music to ragtime, eat your spiritual food with a knife, drape yourself in the flag of the dominant party. In other words, you must be "one hundred per cent" crowd man.

The effect of all this upon the individual is that he is permitted neither to know nor to belong to himself. He becomes a mere banner toter. He must hold himself ever in readiness to wiggle-waggle in the perpetual Simon-says-thumbs-up game which his crowd is playing. He spends his days playing a part which others have written for him; loses much of his genuineness and courage, and pampers himself with imitation virtues and second-hand truths.

Upon the social peace the effect is equally bad. Unnecessary and meaningless strife is engendered. An idolatry of phrases is enthroned. A silly game of bullying and deception is carried on among contending crowds, national, religious, moral, social. The great truths of patriotism, morality, and religion become hardly more than caricatures—mere

8

instruments of crowds for putting their rivals on the defensive, and securing obeisance from the members of the crowd itself, easily repudiated in the hour of the crowd's victory. The social harmony is menaced by numerous cliques and parties, ranging in size all the way from the nation-crowd down to the smallest sect, each setting out like a band of buccaneers bent upon nothing but its own dominance, and seeking to justify its piratical conduct by time-worn platitudes.

That which is meant by the cry of the Russian Revolution, "All power to the soviets," is peculiar neither to Russia nor to the working class. Such in spirit is the cry of every crowd, for every crowd is, psychologically considered, a soviet. The industrial and political danger of the soviet would amount to little or nothing, were it not for the fact that the modern world is already *spiritually sovietized*. The threatened soviet republic is hardly more than the practical result of a hundred years of crowd-thinking on almost every subject. Whether capitalist or proletarian, reformer or liberal, we have all along been behaving and thinking in soviet fashion. In almost every important matter in life we have ignored Emerson's warning that we must rely upon ourselves, and have permitted ourselves to behave and think as crowds, fastening their labels and dogmas upon our spirits and taking their shibboleths upon our tongues, thinking more of the temporary triumph of our particular sect or party than of the effect of our behavior upon ourselves and others.

There is certainly nothing new in the discovery that our social behavior is not what it ought to be. Mediæval thinkers were as much aware of the fact as we are, but they dismissed the social problem with the simple declaration of the "sinfulness of human nature." Nineteenth-century utilitarians felt that the social problem could be solved by more enlightened and more reasonable behavior on the part of individuals. Recent social psychology—of which the writings of Prof. William McDougall are probably the best example, has abandoned the theory that social behavior is primarily governed by reason or by considerations of utility. A better explanation of social phenomena is found in instinct. It is held that the true motives of social behavior are pugnacity, the instinct of self-appreciation or self-debasement, of sex, gregariousness, and the like. Each instinct with its "affective emotion" becomes organized through various complex reactions to the social environment, into fairly well established "sentiments." These sentiments are held to be the controlling social forces. As McDougall says:

10

We may say then that directly or indirectly the instincts are the prime movers of all human activity; by the conative or impulsive force of some instinct (or of some habit derived from an instinct), every train of thought, however cold and passionless it may seem, is borne along toward its end, and every bodily activity is initiated and sustained. The instinctive impulses determine the ends of all activities and supply the driving-power by which all mental activities are sustained; and all the complex intellectual apparatus of the most highly developed mind is but a means toward those ends, is but the instrument by which these impulses seek their satisfactions. . . . These impulses are the mental forces that maintain and shape all the life of individuals and societies, and in them we are confronted with the central mystery of life and mind and will.

This is all very good so far as it goes. But I confess that I am somewhat at loss to know just what it explains so far as crowd-behavior is concerned Do these instincts and sentiments operate the same under all social conditions? Are some of them suppressed by society and forced to seek their satisfaction in roundabout ways? If so, how? Moreover, I fail to find in present-day social psychology, any more than in the writings of Herbert Spencer, Sumner, Ward, and others, any clear distinction between the characteristic behavior of crowds and other forms of social activity. Only the school of Le Bon has shown any definite appreciation of these facts. It is to Le Bon, therefore, in spite of the many and just criticisms of his work, that we must turn for a discussion of the crowd as a problem apart from social psychology in general. Le Bon saw that the mind of the crowd demanded special psychological study, but many of the psychological principles which he used in solving the problem were inadequate to the task. Certain of his conclusions were, therefore, erroneous. Since the close of the nineteenth century, however, psychology has gained much insight into the secret springs of human activity. Possibly the most significant achievement in the history of this science is Freud's work in analytical psychology.

So much light has been thrown upon the unconscious by Freud and other analytical psychologists, that psychology in all its branches is beginning to take some of Freud's discoveries into account. Strictly speaking, psychoanalysis is a therapeutic method. It has, however, greatly enriched our knowledge of mental pathology, and thus much of its data has become indispensable to general psychology and to social psychology in particular.

In his book the *Interpretation of Dreams*, Freud has shown that there exist in the wish-fulfilling mechanisms of dream formation certain definite laws. These laws undoubtedly underlie and determine also many of our crowd-ideas, creeds, conventions, and social ideals. In his book, *Totem and Taboo*, Freud has himself led the way to the application of the analytical psychology to the customs and ideas of primitive groups. I am sure that we shall find, as we proceed, that with the analytical method we shall gain an entirely new insight into the causes and meaning of the behavior of crowds.

II

HOW CROWDS ARE FORMED

IN his well-known work on the psychology
of the crowd Le Bon noted the fact that
the unconscious plays a large part in determining the behavior of crowds. But he is not
clear in his use of the term "unconscious."
In fact, as Graham Wallas justly points out,
his terminology is very loose indeed. Le Bon
seems to have made little or no attempt to
discover in detail the processes of this unconscious. In company with most psychologists
of his time, he based his explanation upon the
theory of "suggestion and imitation." He
saw in the unconscious merely a sort of
mystical "common humanity," from which he
derived his—also mystical—idea of a common
crowd-mind which each individual in the
crowd in some unexplained manner shared.
He says:

The most striking peculiarity presented by a psychological crowd is the following: Whoever be the individuals that compose it, however like or unlike be their
mode of life, their occupations, their character or their

intelligence, the fact that they have been transformed
into a crowd puts them in possession of a sort of collective mind which makes them feel, think, and act in
a manner quite different from that in which each individual of them would feel, think, and act were he in
a state of isolation. . . .

It is easy to prove how much the individual forming
part of a crowd differs from the isolated individual, but
it is less easy to discover the causes of this difference.

To obtain, at any rate, a glimpse of them it is necessary in the first place to call to mind the truth established by modern psychology, that unconscious phenomena play an altogether preponderating part, not
only in organic life, but also in the operations of intelligence. . . . Our conscious acts are the outcome of an
unconscious substratum created in the mind in the
main by heredity. This substratum consists of innumerable characteristics handed down from generation
to generation which constitute the genius of the race. . . .

It is more especially with respect to those unconscious elements which constitute the genius of a race
that all the individuals belonging to it resemble each
other. . . . It is precisely these general qualities of character, governed by forces of which we are unconscious and
possessed by the majority of normal individuals of a
race in much the same degree—it is precisely these
qualities, I say, that in crowds become common property. In the collective mind the intellectual aptitudes
of the individuals, and in consequence their individuality, are weakened. The heterogeneous is swamped in
the homogeneous and the unconscious qualities obtain
the upper hand.

It may safely be said, I think, that this
assumed impersonal collective mind of the
crowd has no existence in a sound psychology.

People's minds show, of course, innumerable mutual influences, but they do not fuse and run together. They are in many respects very similar, but similarity is not identity, even when people are crowded together. Our author has doubtless borrowed here rather uncritically from Herbert Spencer's organic conception of society—his later statement, not quoted here, that the alleged merging of the heterogeneous in the homogeneous would logically imply a regression to a lower stage in evolution, is another bit of Spencerian jargon commonly accepted in Le Bon's day.

When, however, Graham Wallas, in *The Great Society*, states that Le Bon is not "himself clear whether he means that crowds have no collective consciousness, or that every individual in a crowd is completely unconscious," it seems to me that Wallas is a little unfair. Neither Le Bon nor the relation of the unconscious to the crowd-mind may be dismissed in Wallas's apparently easy manner. Le Bon has established two points which I think cannot be successfully denied: first, that the crowd is essentially a psychological phenomenon, people behaving differently in a crowd from the way they behave when isolated; and second, that the unconscious has something to do with crowd-thinking and acting.

Wallas says of Le Bon:

16

HOW CROWDS ARE FORMED

Tarde and Le Bon were Frenchmen brought up on vivid descriptions of the Revolution and themselves apprehensive of the spread of socialism. Political movements which were in large part carried out by men conscious and thoughtful, though necessarily ill informed, seemed therefore to them as they watched them from the outside to be due to the blind and unconscious impulses of masses "incapable both of reflection and of reasoning."

There is some truth in this criticism. In spite of the attempt of the famous author of crowd-psychology to give us a really scientific explanation of crowd-phenomena, his obviously conservative bias robs his work of much of its power to convince. We find here, just as in the case of Gobineau, Nietzsche, Faguet, Conway, and other supporters of the aristocratic idea, an a priori principle of distrust of the common people as such. In many passages Le Bon does not sufficiently distinguish between the crowd and the masses. Class and mass are opposed to each other as though, due to their superior reasoning powers, the classes were somehow free from the danger of behaving as crowd. This is of course not true. Any class may behave and think as a crowd—in fact it usually does so in so far as its class interests are concerned. Anyone who makes a study of the public mind in America to-day will find that the phenomena of the crowd-mind are not at all confined to movements within the working class or so-called common people.

It has long been the habit of conservative writers to identify the crowd with the proletariat and then to feel that the psychology of the situation could be summed up in the statement that the crowd was simply the creature of passion and blind emotion. The psychology which lies back of such a view— if it is psychology rather than class prejudice —is the old intellectualism which sought to isolate the intellect from the emotional nature and make the true mental life primarily a knowledge affair. The crowd, therefore, since it was regarded as an affair of the emotions, was held to be one among many instances of the natural mental inferiority of the common people, and a proof of their general unfitness for self-government.

I do not believe that this emotional theory is the true explanation of crowd-behavior. It cannot be denied that people in a crowd become strangely excited. But it is not only in crowds that people show emotion. Feeling, instinct, impulse, are the dynamic of all mental life. The crowd doubtless inhibits as many emotions as it releases. Fear is conspicuously absent in battle, pity in a lynching mob. Crowds are notoriously anæsthetic toward the finer values of art, music, and poetry. It may even be argued that the feelings of the crowd are dulled, since it is only the exaggerated, the obvious, the cheaply sentimental, which easily moves it.

There was a time when insanity was also regarded as excessive emotion. The insane man was one who raved, he was mad. The word "crazy" still suggests the condition of being "out of one's mind"—that is, driven by irrational emotion. Psychiatry would accept no such explanation to-day. Types of insanity are distinguished, not with respect to the mere amount of emotional excitement they display, but in accordance with the patient's whole psychic functioning. The analyst looks for some mechanism of controlling ideas and their relation to impulses which are operating in the unconscious. So with our understanding of the crowd-mind. Le Bon is correct in maintaining that the crowd is not a mere aggregation of people. *It is a state of mind.* A peculiar psychic change must happen to a group of people before they become a crowd. And as this change is not merely a release of emotion, neither is it the creation of a collective mind by means of imitation and suggestion. My thesis is that *the crowd-mind is a phenomenon which should best be classed with dreams, delusions, and the various forms of automatic behavior*. The controlling ideas of the crowd are the result neither of reflection nor of "suggestion," but are akin to what, as we shall see later, the psychoanalysts term "complexes." The crowd-self—if I may speak of it in this way—is analogous in many respects to "compulsion neurosis," "somnambulism," or "paranoiac episode." Crowd ideas are "fixations"; they are always symbolic; they are always related to something repressed in the unconscious. They are what Doctor Adler would call "fictitious guiding lines."

There is a sense in which all our thinking consists of symbol and fiction. The laws, measurements, and formulas of science are all as it were "shorthand devices"—instruments for relating ourselves to reality, rather than copies of the real. The "truth" of these working ideas is demonstrated in the satisfactoriness of the results to which they lead us. If by means of them we arrive at desired and desirable adaptations to and within our environment, we say they are verified. If, however, no such verification is reached, or the result reached flatly contradicts our hypothesis, the sane thinker holds his conclusions in abeyance, revises his theories, or candidly gives them up and clings to the real as empirically known.

Suppose now that a certain hypothesis, or "fiction," instead of being an instrument for dealing with external reality, is unconsciously designed as a refuge from the real. Suppose it is a symbolic compromise among conflicting desires in the individual's unconscious of which he cannot rid himself. Suppose it is a disguised expression of motives which the individual as a civilized being cannot admit to his own consciousness. Suppose it is a fiction necessary to keep up one's ego consciousness or self-appreciative feeling without which either he or his world would instantly become valueless. In these latter cases the fiction is not and cannot be, without outside help, modified by the reality of experience. The complex of ideas becomes a closed system, a world in and of itself. Conflicting facts of experience are discounted and denied by all the cunning of an insatiable, unconscious will. The fiction then gets itself substituted for the true facts of experience; the individual has "lost the function of the real." He no longer admits its disturbing elements as correctives. He has become mentally unadjusted —pathological.

Most healthy people doubtless would on analysis reveal themselves as nourishing fictions of this sort, more or less innocent in their effects. It is possible that it is by means of such things that the values of living are maintained for us all. But with the healthy these fictions either hover about the periphery of our known world as shadowy and elusive inhabitants of the inaccessible, or else they are socially acceptable as religious convention, race pride, ethical values, personal ambition, class honor, etc. The fact that so much of the ground of our valuations, at least so far as these affect our self-appreciation, is explicable by psychologists as "pathological" in origin need not startle us. William James in his *Varieties of Religious Experience*, you will remember, took the ground that in judging of matters of this kind, it is not so much by their origins—even admitting the pathological as a cause—but by their fruits that we shall know them. There are "fictions" which are neither innocent nor socially acceptable in their effects on life and character. Many of our crowd-phenomena belong, like paranoia, to this last class.

As I shall try to show later, the common confusion of the crowd with "society" is an error. The crowd is a social phenomenon only in the sense that it affects a number of persons at the same time. As I have indicated, people may be highly social without becoming a crowd. They may meet, mingle, associate in all sorts of ways, and organize and cooperate for the sake of common ends—in fact, the greater part of our social life might normally have nothing in common with crowd-behavior. Crowd-behavior is pseudo-social —if social organizations be regarded as a means to the achievement of realizable goods.

The phenomena which we call the crowd-mind, instead of being the outgrowth of the directly social, are social only in the sense that all mental life has social significance; they are rather the result of forces hidden in the personal and unconscious psyche of the members of the crowd, forces which are merely *released* by social gatherings of a certain sort.

Let us notice what happens in a public meeting as it develops into a crowd, and see if we can trace some of the steps of the process. Picture a large meeting-hall, fairly well filled with people. Notice first of all what sort of interest it is which as a rule will most easily bring an assemblage of people together. It need not necessarily be a matter of great importance, but it must be something which catches and challenges attention without great effort. It is most commonly, therefore, an *issue* of some sort. I have seen efforts made in New York to hold mass meetings to discuss affairs of the very greatest importance, and I have noted the fact that such efforts usually fail to get out more than a handful of specially interested persons, no matter how well advertised, if the subject to be considered happens not to be of a controversial nature. I call especial attention to this fact because later we shall see that it is this element of conflict, directly or indirectly, which plays an overwhelming part in the psychology of every crowd.

It is the element of contest which makes baseball so popular. A debate will draw a larger crowd than a lecture. One of the secrets of the large attendance of the forum is the fact that discussion—"talking back"—is permitted and encouraged. The evangelist Sunday undoubtedly owes the great attendance at his meetings in no small degree to the fact that he is regularly expected to abuse some one.

If the matter to be considered is one about which there is keen partisan feeling and popular resentment—if it lends itself to the spectacular personal achievement of one whose name is known, especially in the face of opposition or difficulties—or if the occasion permits of resolutions of protest, of the airing of wrongs, of denouncing abuse of some kind, or of casting statements of external principles in the teeth of "enemies of humanity," then, however trivial the occasion, we may count on it that our assembly will be well attended. Now let us watch the proceedings.

The next thing in importance is the speaker. Preferably he should be an "old war horse," a victor in many battles, and this for a psychological reason which we shall soon examine. Whoever he is, every speaker with any skill knows just when this state of mind which we call "crowd" begins to appear. My work has provided me with rather unusual opportunities for observing this sort of thing. As a regular lecturer and also as director of the forum which meets three nights a week in the great hall of Cooper Union, I have found that the intellectual interest, however intense, and the development of the crowd-spirit are accompanied by wholly different mental processes. Let me add in passing that the audiences which gather at Cooper Union are, on the whole, the most alert, sophisticated, and reflective that I have ever known. I doubt if in any large popular assembly in America general discussion is carried on with such habitual seriousness. When on rare occasions the spirit of the crowd begins to manifest itself—and one can always detect its beginnings before the audience is consciously aware of it—I have noticed that discussion instantly ceases and people begin merely to repeat their creeds and hurl cant phrases at one another. All then is changed, though subtly. There may be laughter as at first; but it is different. Before, it was humorous and playful, now there is a note of hostility in it. It is laughter *at* some one or something. Even the applause is changed. It is more frequent. It is more vigorous, and instead of showing mere approval of some sentiment, it becomes a means of showing the numerical strength of a group

3

of believers of some sort. It is as if those who applaud were unconsciously seeking to reveal to themselves and others that there is a multitude on their side.

I have heard the most exciting and controversial subjects discussed, and seen the discussion listened to with the intensest difference of opinion, and all without the least crowd-phenomena—so long as the speaker refrained from indulging in generalities or time-worn forms of expression. So long as the matter discussed requires close and sustained effort of attention, and the method of treatment is kept free from anything which savors of ritual, even the favorite dogmas of popular belief may be discussed, and though the interest be intense, it will remain critical and the audience does not become a crowd. But let the most trivial bit of bathos be expressed in rhythmical cadences and in platitudinous terms, and the most intelligent audience will react as a crowd. Crowd-making oratory is almost invariably platitudinous. In fact, we think as a crowd only in platitudes, propaganda, ritual, dogma, and symbol. Crowd-ideas are ready-made, they possess finality and universality. They are fixed. They do not develop. They are ends in themselves. Like the obsessions of the insane, there is a deadly inevitability in the logic of them. They are "compulsions."

During the time of my connection with the

26

HOW CROWDS ARE FORMED

Cooper Union Forum, we have not had a crowd-demonstration in anything more than an incipient form. The best laboratory for the study of such a phenomenon is the political party convention, the mass meeting, or the religious revival. The orators who commonly hold forth at such gatherings know intuitively the functional value of bathos, ridicule, and platitude, and it is upon such knowledge that they base the success of their careers in "getting the crowd." The noisy "demonstrations" which it has of late become the custom to stage as part of the rigmarole of a national party convention have been cited as crowning examples of the stupidity and excess of crowd enthusiasm. But this is a mistake. Anyone who has from the gallery witnessed one or more of these mock "stampedes" will agree that they are exhibitions of endurance rather than of genuine enthusiasm or of true crowd-mindedness. They are so obviously manipulated and so deliberately timed that they can hardly be regarded as true crowd-movements at all. They are chiefly interesting as revelations of the general insincerity of the political life of this republic.

True crowd-behavior requires an element of spontaneity—at least on the part of the crowd. And we have abundant examples of this in public meetings of all sorts. As the audience becomes crowd, the speaker's cadence becomes more marked, his voice more oracular, his gestures more emphatic. His message becomes a recital of great abstract "principles." The purely obvious is held up as transcendental. Interest is kept upon just those aspects of things which can be grasped with least effort by all. Emphasis is laid upon those thought processes in which there is greatest natural uniformity. The general, abstract, and superficial come to be exalted at the expense of that which is unique and personal. Forms of thought are made to stand as objects of thinking.

It is clear that such meaning as there is in those abstract names, "Justice," "Right," "Liberty," "Peace," "Glory," "Destiny," etc., or in such general phrases as "Brotherly Love," "Grand and Glorious," "Public Weal," "Common Humanity," and many others, must vary with each one's personal associations. Popular orators deal only with the greatest common denominator of the meaning of these terms—that is, only those elements which are common to the associations of all. Now the common associations of words and phrases of this general nature are very few—hardly more than the bare sound of the words, plus a vague mental attitude or feeling of expectancy, a mere turning of the eyes of the mind, as it were, in a certain direction into empty space. When, for instance, I try now to leave out of the content of "justice" all my personal associations and concrete experiences, I can discover no remaining content beyond a sort of grand emptiness, with the intonations of the word booming in my auditory centers like the ringing of a distant bell. As "public property," the words are only a sort of worn banknote, symbols of many meanings and intentions like my own, deposited in individual minds. Interesting as these personal deposits are, and much as we are mutually interested by them and moved to harmonious acting and speaking, it is doubtful if more than the tiniest fragment of what we each mean by "justice" can ever be communicated. The word is a convenient instrument in adjusting our conduct to that of others, and when such adjustment seems to meet with mutual satisfaction we say, "That is just." But the just thing is always a concrete situation. And the general term "justice" is simply a combination of sounds used to indicate the class of things we call just. In itself it is but a form with the content left out. And so with all other such abstractions.

Now if attention can be directed to this imaginary and vague "meaning for everybody"—which is really the meaning for nobody—and so directed that the associations with the unique in personal experience are blocked, these abstractions will occupy the whole field of consciousness. The mind will yield to any connection which is made among them almost automatically. As conscious attention is cut away from the psyche as a whole, the objects upon which it is centered will appear to have a reality of their own. They become a closed system, perfectly logical it may be in itself, but with the fatal logic commonly found in paranoia—the fiction may become more real than life itself. It may be substituted, while the spell is on, for the world of actual experience. And just as the manifest content of a dream is, according to Freud, the condensed and distorted symbol of latent dream-thoughts and desires in the unconscious, so, in the case we are discussing, the unconscious invests these abstract terms with its own peculiar meanings. They gain a tremendous, though undefined, importance and an irresistible compelling power.

Something like the process I have described occurs when the crowd appears. People are translated to a different world—that is, a different sense of the real. The speaker is transfigured to their vision. His words take on a mysterious importance; something tremendous, eternal, superhuman is at stake. Commonplace jokes become irresistibly amusing. Ordinary truths are wildly applauded. Dilemmas stand clear with all middle ground brushed away. No statement now needs

30

qualification. All thought of compromise is abhorrent. Nothing now must intervene to rob these moments of their splendid intensity. As James once said of drunkenness, "Everything is just utterly utter." They who are not for us are against us.

The crowd-mind consists, therefore, first of all, of a disturbance of the function of the real. *The crowd is the creature of Belief.* Every crowd has its peculiar "illusions," ideals, dreams. It maintains its existence as a crowd just so long as these crowd-ideas continue to be held by practically all the members of the group—so long, in fact, as such ideas continue to hold attention and assent to the exclusion of ideas and facts which contradict them.

I am aware of the fact that we could easily be led aside at this point into endless metaphysical problems. It is not our purpose to enter upon a discussion of the question, what is the real world? The problem of the real is by no means so simple as it appears "to common sense." Common sense has, however, in practical affairs, its own criteria, and beyond these it it not necessary for us now to stray. The "illusions" of the crowd are almost never illusions in the psychological sense. They are not false perceptions of the objects of sense. They are rather akin to the delusions and fixed ideas commonly found in paranoia. The man in the street does not ordinarily require the technique either of metaphysics or of psychiatry in order to characterize certain individuals as "crazy." The "crazy" man is simply unadjustable in his speech and conduct. His ideas may be real to him, just as the color-blind man's sensations of color may be as real as those of normal people, but they won't work, and that is sufficient.

It is not so easy to apply this criterion of the real to our crowd-ideas. Social realities are not so well ordered as the behavior of the forces of nature. Things moral, religious, and political are constantly in the making. The creative role which we all play here is greater than elsewhere in our making of reality. When most of our neighbors are motivated by certain ideas, those ideas become part of the social environment to which we must adjust ourselves. In this sense they are "real," however "crazy." Every struggle-group and faction in society is constantly striving to establish its ideas as controlling forces in the social reality. The conflicts among ideals are therefore in a sense conflicts within the real. Ideas and beliefs which seek their verification in the character of the results to which they lead, may point to very great changes in experience, and so long as the believer takes into account the various elements with which he has to deal, he has not lost his hold upon reality. But when one's beliefs or principles become ends in themselves, when by themselves they seem to constitute an order of being which is more interesting than fact, when the believer saves his faith only by denying or ignoring the things which contradict him, when he strives not to verify his ideas but to "vindicate" them, the ideas so held are pathological. The obsessions of the paranoiac are of this sort. We shall see later that these ideas have a meaning, though the conscious attention of the patient is systematically diverted from that meaning. Crowd-ideas are similar. The reason why their pathology is not more evident is the fact that they are simultaneously entertained by so great a number of people.

There are many ideas in which our faith is sustained chiefly by the knowledge that everyone about us also believes them. Belief on such ground has commonly been said to be due to imitation or suggestion. These do play a large part in determining all our thinking, but I can see no reason why they should be more operative in causing the crowd-mind than in other social situations. In fact, the distinctive phenomena which I have called crowd-ideas clearly show that other causes are at work.

Among civilized people, social relationships

make severe demands upon the individual. Primitive impulses, unchecked eroticism, tendencies to perversions, and antisocial demands of the ego which are in us all, are constantly inhibited, resisted, controlled and diverted to socially acceptable ends. The savage in us is "repressed," his demands are so habitually denied that we learn to keep him down, for the most part, without conscious effort. We simply cease to pay attention to his gnawing desires. We become decently respectable members of society largely at the expense of our aboriginal nature. But the primitive in us does not really die. It asserts itself harmlessly in dreams. Psychoanalysis has revealed the fact that every dream is the realization of some desire, usually hidden from our conscious thought by our habitual repression. For this reason the dream work consists of symbols. The great achievement of Freud is the technique which enables the analyst to interpret this symbolism so that his own unconscious thought and desire are made known to the subject. The dream is harmless and is normally utilized by the unconscious ego because during sleep we cannot move. If one actually did the things he dreamed, a thing which happens in various somnambulisms, the dream would become anything but harmless. Every psychosis is really a dramatized dream of this sort.

34

Now as it is the social which demands the repression of our primitive impulses, it is to be expected that the unconscious would on certain occasions make use of this same social in order to realize its primitive desires. There are certain mental abnormalities, such as dementia præcox, in which the individual behaves in a wholly antisocial manner, simply withdrawing into himself. *In the crowd the primitive ego achieves its wish by actually gaining the assent and support of a section of society. The immediate social environment is all pulled in the same direction as the unconscious desire.* A similar unconscious impulse motivates each member of the crowd. It is as if all at once an unspoken agreement were entered into whereby each member might let himself go, on condition that he approved the same thing in all the rest. Of course such a thing cannot happen consciously. Our normal social consciousness would cause us each to resist, let us say, an exhibition of cruelty— in our neighbors, and also in ourselves. The impulse must therefore be disguised.

The term "unconscious" in the psychology of the crowd does not, of course, imply that the people in the crowd are not aware of the fact that they are lynching a negro or demanding the humiliation or extermination of certain of their fellows. Everybody is perfectly aware of what is being said and done; only *the moral*

significance of the thing is changed. The deed or sentiment, instead of being disapproved, appears to be demanded, by moral principle, by the social welfare, by the glory of the state, etc. What is unconscious is the fact that the social is actually being twisted around into giving approval of the things which it normally forbids. Every crowd considers that it is vindicating some sacred principle. The more bloody and destructive the acts to which it is impelled, the more moral are its professions. Under the spell of the crowd's logic certain abstract principles lead inevitably to the characteristic forms of crowd-behavior. They seem to glorify such acts, to make heroes and martyrs of those who lead in their performance.

The attention of everyone is first centered on the abstract and universal, as I have indicated. The repressed wish then unconsciously gives to the formulas which the crowd professes a meaning different from that which appears, yet unconsciously associated with it. This unconscious meaning is of course an impulse to act. But the motive professed is not the real motive.

Normally our acts and ideas are corrected by our social environment. But in a crowd our test of the real fails us, because, since the attention of all near us is directed in the same way as our own, the social environment for the time fails to check us.   As William James said:

> The sense that anything we think is unreal can only come when that thing is contradicted by some other thing of which we think.   Any object which remains uncontradicted is *ipso facto* believed and posited as "absolute reality."

Our immediate social environment is all slipping along with us. It no longer contradicts the thing we want to believe, and, unconsciously, want to do. As the uncontradicted idea is, for the time, reality, so is it a motor impulse. The only normal reason why we do not act immediately upon any one of our ideas is that action is inhibited by ideas of a contradictory nature. As crowd, therefore, we find ourselves moving in a fictitious system of ideas uncritically accepted as real— not as in dreams realizing our hidden wishes, merely in imagination, but also impelled to act them out in much the way that the psychoneurotic is impelled to act out the fixed ideas which are really the symbols of his suppressed wish. In other words, *a crowd is a device for indulging ourselves in a kind of temporary insanity by all going crazy together.*

Of the several kinds of crowds, I have selected for our discussion the mass meeting, because we are primarily interested in the *ideas* which dominate the crowd. The same essential psychological elements are also found in the street crowd or mob. Serious mob outbreaks seldom occur without mass meetings, oratory, and propaganda. Sometimes, as in the case of the French Revolution and of the rise of the soviets in Russia, the mass meetings are held in streets and public places. Sometimes, as, for instance, the crowds in Berlin when Germany precipitated the World War, a long period of deliberate cultivation of such crowd-ideas as happen to be advantageous to the state precedes. There are instances, such as the Frank case, which brought unenviable fame to Georgia, when no mass meeting seems to have been held. It is possible that in this instance, however, certain newspapers, and also the trial—which, as I remember, was held in a theater and gave an ambitious prosecuting attorney opportunity to play the role of mob leader—served the purpose of the mass meeting.

The series of outbreaks in New York and other cities, shortly after the War, between the socialists and certain returned soldiers, seem to have first occurred quite unexpectedly, as do the customary negro lynchings in the South. In each case I think it will be found that the complex of crowd-ideas had been previously built up in the unconscious. A deep-seated antagonism had been unconsciously associated with the self-appreciative feelings of a number of individuals, all of which found justification in the consciousness of these persons in the form of devotion to principle, loyalty, moral enthusiasm, etc. I suspect that under many of our professed principles there lurk elements of unconscious sadism and masochism. All that is then required is an occasion, some casual incident which will so direct the attention of a number of these persons that they provide one another temporarily with a congenial social environment. In the South this mob complex is doubtless formed out of race pride, a certain unconscious eroticism, and will to power, which unfortunately has too abundant opportunity to justify itself as moral indignation. With the returned soldiers the unconscious desires were often rather thinly disguised— primitive impulses to violence which had been aroused and hardly satisfied by the war, a wish to exhibit themselves which found its opportunity in the knowledge that their lawlessness would be applauded in certain influential quarters, a dislike of the nonconformist, the foreign, and the unknown, which took the outward form of a not wholly unjustifiable resentment toward the party which had to all appearances unpatriotically opposed our entrance into the war.

Given a psychic situation of this nature, the steps by which it leads to mob violence are much alike in all cases. All together they simply amount to a process of like direction of the attention of a sufficient number of persons so affected as to produce a temporary social environment in which the unconscious impulses may be released with mutual approval. The presence of the disliked object or person gains general attention. At first there is only curiosity; then amusement; there is a bantering of crude witticisms; then ridicule. Soon the joking turns to insults. There are angry exclamations. A blow is struck. There is a sudden rush. The blow, being the act which the members of the crowd each unconsciously wished to do, gains general approval, "it is a blow for righteousness"; a "cause" appears. Casually associated persons at once become a group, brought together, of course, by their interest in vindicating the principles at stake. The mob finds itself suddenly doing things which its members did not know they had ever dreamed of.

Different as this process apparently is from that by which a meeting is turned into a crowd by an orator, I think it will be seen that the two are essentially alike.

Thus far we have been considering crowd-movements which are local and temporary— casual gatherings, which, having no abiding reason for continued association, soon dissolve into their individual elements. Frequently, after participating in such a movement, the individual, on returning to his

habitual relations, "comes to." He wonders
what the affair was all about. In the light
of his re-established control ideas—he will call
it "reason"—the unconscious impulses are
again repressed; he may look with shame and
loathing upon yesterday's orgy. Acts which
he would ordinarily disapprove in his neighbors, he now disapproves in himself. If the
behavior of the crowd has not been particularly atrocious and inexcusable to ordinary
consciousness, the reaction is less strong. The
voter after the political campaign merely
"loses interest." The convert in the revival
"backslides." The striker returns to work
and is soon absorbed by the daily routine of
his task. The fiery patriot, after the war, is
surprised to find that his hatred of the enemy
is gradually waning. Electors who have been
swept by a wave of enthusiasm for "reform"
and have voted for a piece of ill-considered restrictive legislation easily lapse into indifference, and soon look with unconcern or
amusement upon open violations of their own
enactments. There is a common saying that
the public has a short memory. Pick up an
old newspaper and read about the great movements and causes which were only a short
time ago stirring the public mind, many of
them are now dead issues. But they were
not answered by argument; we simply "got
over" them.

Not all crowd-movements, however, are local and temporary. There are passing moments of crowd-experience which are often too sweet to lose. The lapse into everyday realism is like "falling from grace." The crowd state of mind strives often to keep itself in countenance by perpetuating the peculiar social-psychic conditions in which it can operate. There are certain forms of the ego consciousness which are best served by the fictions of the crowd. An analogy here is found in paranoia, where the individual's morbid fixed ideas are really devices for the protection of his self-esteem. The repressed infantile psyche which exists in us all, and in certain neurotics turns back and attaches itself to the image of the parent, finds also in the crowd a path for expression. It provides a perpetual interest in keeping the crowd-state alive. Notice how invariably former students form alumni associations, and returned soldiers at once effect permanent organizations; persons who have been converted in one of Mr. Sunday's religious campaigns do the same thing—indeed there are associations of all sorts growing out of these exciting moments in people's common past experience, the purpose of which is mutually to recall the old days and aid one another in keeping alive the enlarged self-feeling.

In addition to this, society is filled with

what might be called "struggle groups"
organized for the survival and dominance of
similarly constituted or situated people. Each
group has its peculiar interests, economic,
spiritual, racial, etc., and each such interest
is a mixture of conscious and unconscious purposes. These groups become sects, cults, partisan movements, class struggles. They develop propaganda, ritual, orthodoxies, dogma,
all of which are hardly anything more than
stereotyped systems of crowd-ideas. These
systems differ from those of the neurosis in
that the former are less idiosyncratic, but
they undoubtedly perform much the same
function. The primary aim of every such
crowd is to keep itself together as a crowd.
Hardly less important is the desire of its
members to dominate over all outsiders. The
professed purpose is to serve some cause or
principle of universal import. Thus the crowd
idealizes itself as an end, makes sanctities of
its own survival values, and holds up its ideals
to all men, demanding that every knee shall
bow and every tongue confess—which is to
say, that the crowd believes in its own future
supremacy, the members of the group knowing
that such a belief has survival value. This
principle is used by every politician in pre-
dicting that his party is bound to win at the
next election.

Hence the crowd is a device by which the

individual's "right" may be baptized "right-eousness" in general, and this personality by putting on impersonality may rise again to new levels of self-appreciation. He "belongs to something," something "glorious" and deathless. He himself may be but a miserable clod, but the glory of his crowd reflects upon him. Its expected triumph he already shares. It gives him back his lost sense of security. As a good crowd man, true believer, loyal citizen, devoted member, he has regained something of his early innocence. In other members he has new brothers and sisters. In the finality of his crowd-faith there is escape from responsibility and further search. He is willing to be commanded. He is a child again. He has transferred his repressed infantilism from the lost family circle to the crowd. There is a very real sense in which the crowd stands to his emotional life *in loco parentis*.

It is to be expected, therefore, that wherever possible the crowd-state of mind will be perpetuated. Every sort of device will be used to keep the members of the crowd from coming to. In almost every organization and social relationship there will be a tendency on part of the unconscious to behave as crowd. Thus permanent crowds exist on every hand—especially wherever political, moral, or religious ideas are concerned. The general

44

and abstract character of these ideas makes them easily accessible instruments for justifying and screening the unconscious purpose. Moreover it is in just those aspects of our social life where repression is greatest that crowd-thinking is most common, for it is by means of such thinking and behavior that the unconscious seeks evasions and finds its necessary compensations.

The modern man has in the printing press a wonderfully effective means for perpetuating crowd-movements and keeping great masses of people constantly under the sway of certain crowd-ideas. Every crowd-group has its magazines, press agents, and special "literature" with which it continually harangues its members and possible converts. Many books, and especially certain works of fiction of the "best-seller" type, are clearly reading-mob phenomena.

But the leader in crowd-thinking *par excellence* is the daily newspaper. With few exceptions our journals emit hardly anything but crowd-ideas. These great "molders of public opinion," reveal every characteristic of the vulgar mob orator. The character of the writing commonly has the standards and prejudices of the "man in the street." And lest this man's ego consciousness be offended by the sight of anything "highbrow"—that is, anything indicating that there may be a

45

superior intelligence or finer appreciation than his own—newspaper-democracy demands that everything more exalted than the level of the lowest cranial altitude be left out. The average result is a deluge of sensational scandal, class prejudice, and special pleading clumsily disguised with a saccharine smear of the cheapest moral platitude. Consequently, the thinking of most of us is carried on chiefly in the form of crowd-ideas. A sort of public-meeting self is developed in the consciousness of the individual which dominates the personality of all but the reflective few. We editorialize and press-agent ourselves in our inmost musings. Public opinion is manufactured just as brick are made. Possibly a slightly better knowledge of mechanical engineering is required for making public opinion, but the process is the same. Both can be stamped out in the quantity required, and delivered anywhere to order. Our thinking on most important subjects to-day is as little original as the mental processes of the men who write and the machines which print the pages we read and repeat as our own opinions.

Thomas Carlyle was never more sound than when railing at this "paper age." And paper, he wisely asked us to remember, "is made of old rags." Older writers who saw the ragged throngs in the streets were led to identify the mob or crowd with the tattered, illiterate

46

populace. Our mob to-day is no longer merely tramping the streets. We have it at the breakfast table, in the subway, alike in shop and boudoir, and office—wherever, in fact, the newspaper goes. And the raggedness is not exterior, nor is the mob confined to the class of the ill-clad and the poor. The raggedness, and tawdriness have now become spiritual, a universal presence entering into the fabric of nearly all our mental processes.

We have now reached a point from which we can look back over the ground we have traversed and note the points of difference between our view and the well-known theory of Le Bon. The argument of the latter is as follows: (1) From the standpoint of psychology, the crowd, as the term is here defined, is not merely a group of people, it is the appearance within such a group of a special mental condition, or crowd-mind. (2) The sentiments and ideas of all the persons in the gathering take one and the same direction. (3) Conscious personality vanishes. (4) A collective mind is formed: This is Le Bon's "Law of the mental unity of crowds." (5) This collective mind consists in the main of "general qualities of character" which are our common racial inheritance. It is an "unconscious substratum" which in the crowd becomes uppermost, dominating over the unique personal consciousness. (6) Three causes determine the characteristics of the crowd-mind. (a) From purely numerical considerations, the individual acquires a sentiment of invincible power which encourages him in an unrestrained yielding to his instincts. (b) Contagion, or imitation, and (c) hypnotic suggestion cause the individuals in the crowd to become "slaves of all the unconscious activities of the spinal cord." (7) The resulting characteristics of the crowd are (a) a descent of several rungs in the ladder of civilization, (b) a general intellectual inferiority as compared with the isolated individual, (c) loss of moral responsibility, (d) impulsiveness, (e) credulity, (f) exaggeration, (g) intolerance, (h) blind obedience to the leader of the crowd, (i) a mystical emotionalism. (8) The crowd is finally and somewhat inconsistently treated by Le Bon as being identical with the masses, the common people, the herd.

Without pausing to review the criticisms of this argument which were made at the beginning of our discussion, our own view may be summarized as follows: (1) The crowd is not the same as the masses, or any class or gathering of people as such, but is a certain mental condition which may occur simultaneously to people in any gathering or association. (2) This condition is not a "collective mind." It is a release of repressed impulses which is made possible because certain controlling

48

ideas have ceased to function in the immediate
social environment. (3) This modification in
the immediate social environment is the result
of mutual concessions on the part of persons
whose unconscious impulses to do a certain
forbidden thing are similarly disguised as
sentiments which meet with conscious moral
approval. (4) Such a general disguising of
the real motive is a characteristic phenomenon
of dreams and of mental pathology, and occurs
in the crowd by fixing the attention of all
present upon the abstract and general. Attention is thus held diverted from the individual's personal associations, permitting
these associations and their accompanying
impulses to function unconsciously. (5) The
abstract ideas so entertained become symbols
of meanings which are unrecognized; they
form a closed system, like the obsessions of the
paranoiac, and as the whole group are thus
moved in the same direction, the "compulsory" logic of these ideas moves forward without those social checks which normally keep
us within bounds of the real. Hence, acting
and thinking in the crowd become stereotyped and "ceremonial." Individuals move
together like automatons. (6) As the unconscious chiefly consists of that part of our
nature which is habitually repressed by the
social, and as there is always, therefore, an
unconscious resistance to this repressive force,

it follows that the crowd state, like the neurosis, is a mechanism of escape and of compensation. It also follows that the crowd-spirit will occur most commonly in reference to just those social forms where repression is greatest—in matters political, religious, and moral. (7) The crowd-mind is then not a mere excess of emotion on the part of people who have abandoned "reason"; crowd-behavior is in a sense psychopathic and has many elements in common with somnambulism, the compulsion neurosis, and even paranoia. (8) Crowds may be either temporary or permanent in their existence. Permanent crowds, with the aid of the press, determine in greater or less degree the mental habits of nearly everyone. The individual moves through his social world like a popular freshman on a college campus, who is to be "spiked" by one or another fraternity competing for his membership. A host of crowds standing for every conceivable "cause" and "ideal" hover constantly about him, ceaselessly screaming their propaganda into his ears, bullying and cajoling him, pushing and crowding and denouncing one another, and forcing all willy-nilly to line up and take sides with them upon issues and dilemmas which represent the real convictions of nobody.

III

THE CROWD AND THE UNCONSCIOUS

THROUGHOUT the discussion thus far I have been making repeated reference to the psychology of the unconscious, without going into detail any more than was necessary. Let us now take a closer look at some of Freud's discoveries. In this way, what Brill would call the "psychogenesis" of certain characteristic ideas and practices of crowds will be, I think, made clear. Up to this point we have dealt generally with those mental processes by which the crowd is formed. There are certain traits, tendencies, ways of thinking which crowds so uniformly display that one is justified, in want of other explanation, in assuming them to be unconsciously determined. The remarkable blindness of organized crowds to the most obvious of their own performances is so common as to be the regularly expected thing—that is, of crowds other than our own. Long and extensive operations may be carried on for years by crowds whose members repeatedly declare that such things are not being done. The way in which a nation will carefully prepare for war, gradually organizing its whole life on a military basis with tremendous cost and effort, all the while declaring that it is interested only in peace, denying its warlike intentions, and even in the moment of picking a quarrel with its neighbors declare to all the world that it had been wantonly and unexpectedly attacked, is all a matter of general comment. The American colonists, during the decade before the signing of the Declaration of Independence, of course had no conscious thought of separating from Great Britain. Almost to the very last they professed their loyalty to the King; but looking back now it is clear that Independence was the motive all along, and doubtless could not have been achieved more opportunely or with greater finesse if it had been deliberately planned from the start. The Hebrew Scriptures contain a story which illustrates this aspect of crowd-behavior everywhere. The Children of Israel in bondage in Egypt merely wished to go out in the wilderness for a day or so to worship their God. All they asked was religious liberty. How unjust of the authorities to assume they were planning to run away from their masters! You will remember that at the last moment they incidentally borrow some jewelry from their Egyptian neighbors. Of course they will pay it back after their little religious holiday, but . . . later a most unforeseen thing happens to that jewelry, a scandalous thing—it is made into an idol. Does it require that one be a psychologist to infer that it was the unconscious intention all along to use this metal for just that, the first good chance they had—and that, too, notwithstanding repeated prohibitions of idolatry? The motive for borrowing the jewelry is evident.

Certain crowd-movements in America today give marked evidence of this unconscious motivation. Notice how both the radical and reactionary elements behave when, as is frequently the case with both, the crowd-spirit comes over them. Certain radicals, who are fascinated with the idea of the Russian Revolution, are still proclaiming sentiments of human brotherhood, peace, and freedom, while unconsciously they are doing just what their enemies accuse them of—playing with the welcome ideas of violence, class war, and proletarian dictatorship. And conservative crowds, while ostensibly defending American traditions and ideals against destructive foreign influence, are with their own hands daily desecrating many of the finest things which America has given to the world in its struggle of more than a century for freedom and justice. Members of each crowd, while blissfully unaware of the incompatibility of their own motives and professions, have no illusions about those of the counter-crowd. Each crowd sees in the professions of its antagonist convincing proof of the insincerity and hypocrisy of the other side. To the student of social philosophy both are right and both wrong. All propaganda is lies, and every crowd is a deceiver, but its first and worst deception is that of itself. This self-deception is a necessary step in crowd-formation and is a *sine qua non* of becoming a crowd. It is only necessary for members of a crowd to deceive themselves and one another for the crowd-mind to function perfectly; I doubt if they are often successful in deceiving anybody else. It was this common crowd-phenomenon of self-deception which led Gobineau and Nietzsche to the conclusion that the common people are liars. But as has been said, the crowd is by no means peculiar to the working class; some of its worst features are exhibited these days among employers, law-makers, and the well-to-do classes. This deception is moreover not really conscious and deliberate. If men deliberately set about to invent lies to justify their behavior I have little doubt that most of them would be clever enough to conjure up something a little more plausible. These naïve and threadbare "hypocrisies" of crowds are a commonplace mechanism of the unconscious. It is interesting to note that the delusions of the paranoiac likewise deceive no one but himself, yet within themselves form a perfectly logical *a priori* system. They also serve the well-understood purpose, like that of crowd-ideas, of keeping their possessor in a certain fixed relation toward portions of his own psychic material. As Brill says, they are "compromise formations."

Those who have read Freud's little book, *Delusion and Dream*, an analysis of a psychological romance written by Wilhelm Jensen, will recall how extensive a fabric of plausibilities a delusion may build up in its defense in order at the same time to satisfy a repressed wish, and keep the true meaning of the subject's acts and thoughts from conscious attention. In the story which Freud has here taken as his subject for study, a young student of archæology has apparently conquered all adolescent erotic interest and has devoted himself whole-heartedly to his science. While at the ruins of ancient Pompeii, he finds a bas-relief containing the figure of a young woman represented in the act of walking with peculiar grace. A cast of this figure he brings home. His interest is curiously aroused. At first this interest appears to be scientific only, then æsthetic, and historical. Finally he builds up about it a complete romance. He becomes restless and very much of a misogynist, and is driven, he knows not why, again to the ruins. Here he actually meets the object of his dreams in the solitude of the excavated city. He allows himself to believe that the once living model of his treasured bas-relief has again come to life. For days he meets and talks with the girl, living all the while in a world of complete unreality, until she finally succeeds in revealing herself as the young woman who lives next door to him. It also appears that in their childhood he and this girl had been playmates, and that in spite of all his conscious indifference to her his unconscious interest was the source of his interest in the bas-relief and the motive which led him to return to Pompeii, where he unconsciously expected to find her. The interesting thing about all this for our present study is the series of devices, fictions, and compromises with reality which this repressed interest made use of while having its way with him, and at the same time resisting whatever might force it upon his conscious attention, where a recognition of its significance might result in a deliberate rejection.

We shall not go into Freud's ingenious analysis of the mental processes at work here. The following passage is sufficient for our purpose:

There is a kind of forgetting which distinguishes itself by the difficulty with which memory is awakened, even by strong appeals, as if a subjective resistance struggled against the revival. Such forgetting has received the name of "repression" in psychopathology . . . about repression we can assert that certainly it does not coincide with the destruction, the obliteration of memory. The repressed material can not of itself break through as memory, but remains potent and effective.

From this, and from what was said in our previous chapter, it is plain that the term "unconscious" as used in psychology does not mean total absence of psychic activity. It refers to thoughts and feelings which have *purposefully* been forgotten — to experiences or impulses to which we do not pay attention nor wish to attend to, but which influence us nevertheless. Everyone of us, when he dreams, has immediate knowledge of the unconscious as here defined. Certainly we pass into unconsciousness when we sleep. Yet something is unquestionably going on inside our heads. One wakens and says, "What strange, or exciting, or delightful dreams I have had!" Bergson says that sleep is due to the relaxing of attention to our environment. Yet in dreams attention is never turned away from ourselves. Possibly instead of the word "unconscious" the term "unattended" might be used with less danger of confusion.

Consciousness is, therefore, not the whole of our psychic activity. Much of our behavior is reflex and automatic. James used to be

5

fond of showing how much even of our higher
psychic activity was reflex in its nature. We
may be conscious of various portions of our
psychic material, but never of all of it at once.
Attention is like a spotlight thrown on a semi-
darkened stage, moving here and there, revealing the figures upon which it is directed in
vivid contrast with the darkly moving objects which animate the regions outside its
circle. A speaker during his discourse will
straighten his tie, make various gestures, and
toy with any object which happens to be lying
on the desk, all without being aware of his
movements, until his attention is called to
the fact. Absent-minded persons habitually
amuse us by frequently performing complete
and rather complex series of actions while
wholly oblivious to what they are doing.
Everyone can recall numerous instances of
absent-mindedness in his own experience.

Now all pathological types of mental life
have in common this quality of absent-mindedness, and it is held that the thing said or done
absent-mindedly has in every instance, even
when normal, a meaning which is unconscious.
But the unconscious or unattended is by no
means confined to the infrequent and the
trivial. As temperament, or character, its
activity is a determining factor in all our
thought and conduct. Dream fancies do not
really cease when we awake; the dream

58

activity goes on all about our conscious thoughts, our associations now hovering near long-forgotten memories, now pulled in the direction of some unrecognized bit of personal conceit, now skipping on tiptoe over something forbidden and wicked and passing across without looking in; only a part of our mental processes ever directly finding expression in our conscious acts and words. The unchosen and the illogical run along with the desired and the logical material, only we have learned not to pay attention to such things. Under all our logical structures there flows a ceaseless stream of dream stuff. Our conscious thought is like little planks of attention laid end to end on the stones which here and there rise above the surface of our thinking. The mind skips across to a desired conclusion, not infrequently getting its feet wet, and, on occasion, upsetting a plank or slipping off and falling in altogether.

We have only to relax our attention a little to enter the world of day dreams, of art, and religion; we can never hold it so rigid as to be wholly rational for long.

Those interested in the general psychology of the unconscious are referred to the writings of such authorities in this field as Freud, Jung, Adler, Dr. A. A. Brill, and Dr. William White. In fact, the literature dealing with psychoanalysis is now so widely read that, unless the reader has received his information about this branch of science from hostile sources alone, it is to be assumed that he has a fairly accurate acquaintance with its general history and theory. We must confine our discussions to those aspects of unconscious behavior which can be shown by analogy with the psychoneurosis to be determinants of crowd-thinking. As the details and technical discussions of psychoanalytical material belong strictly to the psychiatric clinic, any attempt at criticism by the medical layman of the scientific processes by which they are established is of course impossible. Consequently, I have sought to make use of only those principles which are now so well established as to become rather generally accepted commonplaces of psychopathology.

All analysis reveals the fact that the unconscious of the individual is concerned primarily with himself. This is true in the psychosis, and always in dreams. Freud says:

Every dream is absolutely egotistical; in every dream the beloved ego appears, even though it be in a disguised form. The wishes that are realized in dreams are regularly the wishes of this ego; it is only a deceptive appearance if interest in another person is thought to have caused the dream.

Freud then proceeds to give analyses of several dreams in which the naïve egoism of childhood which lies at the core of the unconscious psyche is apparently absent, and shows that in each and every case it is there. The hero of our dreams, notwithstanding all appearances to the contrary, is always ourself.

Brill, in his book, *Psychoanalysis*, says of the neurosis:

Both hysteria and compulsion neurosis belong to the defense neuropsychoses; their symptoms originate through the psychic mechanism of defense, that is, through the attempt to repress a painful idea which was incompatible with the ego of the patient. There is still another more forceful and more successful form of defense wherein the ego misplaces the incompatible idea with its emotions and acts as though the painful idea had never come to pass. When this occurs the person merges into a psychosis which may be called "hallucinatory confusion."

Thus the psychoneurosis is in all its forms, I believe, regarded as a drama of the ego and its inner conflicts. The egoism of the unconscious belongs alike to the normal and the unadjusted. The mental abnormalities appear when the ego seeks to escape some such conflict by means of a closed system of ideas or symbolic acts which will divert attention from the unwelcome psychic material. Adler, in *The Neurotic Constitution*, is even, if possible, more emphatic in affirming the egoism of the unconscious as revealed in neurotics. His thesis is that the mainspring of all the efforts

61

of achievement and the source of all the vicissitudes of the psyche is a desire to be important, or will to "be above," not wholly unlike Nietzsche's theory of the "will to power." The neurosis goes back to some organic defect or other cause of childish humiliation. As a result, the cause of such humiliation, a defective bodily organ, or whatever it may be, gains special attention. The whole psyche is modified in the process of adjustment. In cases where the psyche remains normal, adjustment is achieved through stimulation to extra effort to overcome the disadvantage, as in the triumph of Demosthenes, Byron, Pope.

On the contrary, this disadvantage may result in a fixed feeling of inferiority. Such a feeling may be brought about in the sensitive child by a variety of circumstances, physical facts such as smallness of stature, adenoids, derangements of the alimentary organs, undersized genitals, homeliness of feature, or any physical deformity or weakness; again by such circumstances as domineering parents or older brothers and sisters. The child then thinks always of himself. He forms the habit of comparing himself with others. He creates, as a protection against the recognition of this feeling of inferiority, what Adler calls the "masculine protest."

The feeling which the individual has of his own inferiority, incompetency, the realization of his smallness, of his weakness, of his uncertainty, thus becomes the appropriate working basis which, because of the intrinsically associated feelings of pleasure and pain, furnishes the inner impulse to advance toward an imaginary goal. . . .

In all similar attempts (and the human psyche is full of them), it is the question of the introduction of an unreal and abstract scheme into actual life. . . . No matter from what angle we observe the psychic development of a normal or neurotic person, he is always found ensnared in the meshes of his particular fiction—a fiction from which the neurotic is unable to find his way back to reality and in which he believes, while the sound and normal person utilizes it for the purpose of reaching a definite goal . . . the thing which impels us all, and especially the neurotic and the child, to abandon the direct path of induction and deduction and use such devices as the schematic fiction, originates in the feeling of uncertainty, and is the craving for security, the final purpose of which is to escape from the feeling of inferiority in order to ascend to the full height of the ego consciousness, to complete manliness, to attain the ideal of being "above." . . .

Even our judgments concerning the value of things are determined according to the standard of the imaginary goal, not according to "real" feelings or pleasurable sensations.

That repressed sexuality plays an important part in the conflicts of the ego is well known to all who are acquainted with analytical psychology. According to Freud, the sexual impulse dates from earliest childhood and is an essential element in every stage of self-appreciation. A summary of the process by which the infantile ego develops to maturity is as follows: The child is by nature "polymorphous perverse"—that is, both physically and psychically he possesses elements which in the mature individual would be considered perversions. Physiologically, what are known as "erogenous zones"—tissue which is capable of what in mature life is sexual excitation—are diffused through the organism. As the child passes through the "latent period" of later childhood and adolescence, these "erogenous zones" are concentrated as it were in the organs which are to serve the purpose of reproduction. If for any reason this process of concentration is checked, and remains in later life incomplete, the mature individual will be afflicted with certain tendencies to sex perversion.

Similarly the psychosexual passes through a metamorphosis in normal development. The erotic interest of the child, at first quite without any object at all, is soon attached to one or the other of the parents, then, in the "narcissus period" is centered upon the individual himself, after which, normally, but not without some storm and stress, it becomes detached and capable of "object love"—that is, love of a person of the opposite sex. This psychic process is by no means a smooth and easy matter. It is attended at every stage with such dangers that a very large number of people never achieve it entire. Various kinds of "shock" and wrong educational influence, or overindulgence on the part of the parents, may cause the psychosexual interest of the ego—or "libido"—to remain "fixed" at some point in its course. It may retain vestiges of its early undifferentiated stage, appearing then in the perverted forms of "masochism" —sexual enjoyment of self-torture—or "sadism"—sexual pleasure in torturing others. Or the libido may remain fixed upon the parent, rendering the individual in some degree incapable of a normal mature love life. He has never quite succeeded in severing his infantile attachment to his mother and transferring his interest to the world of social relations and mature experiences. If he meets with a piece of misfortune, he is likely to seek imaginary security and compensation by a "regression" of the libido and a revival of childlike affection for the mother image. As this return is, in maturity, unconsciously resisted by the horror of incest, a conflict results. The individual then develops certain mechanisms or "complex formations" in defense of his ego against this painful situation. The withdrawal of the libido from the ordinary affairs of life renders the latter valueless. Thoughts of death and like compulsory mechanisms ensue. The patient has become a neurotic.

Psychoanalysts make much of this latter situation. They term it the "Œdipus complex." They assert that in its severer forms it is a common feature of psychoneurosis, while in less marked form, according to Jung, it underlies, and is the real explanation of the "birth of tragedy," being also the meaning of much religious symbolism, including the Divine Drama of Christian tradition. It is not, therefore, only the psychoneurotic whose unconscious takes the form of the "Œdipus complex." Under certain conditions it is manifest in normal people. I have already indicated that the crowd is one of those conditions, and shall have something a little more specific to say about this later on.

Again the growing libido may become fixed in the "narcissus stage." Between the period of love of parents and object love, the adolescent youth passes through a period when he is "in love with himself." The fact that many people remain in some measure fixed in this period of their development is not surprising when we remember that self-feeling occupies a central place in the unconscious at all times. Many of the world's greatest men have doubtless been characters in which there was a slightly more than average fixation at this point. Inordinate ambition is, I should say, an evidence of such a fixation. If one possesses great natural ability he may under such circumstances be able to forge ahead to his goal, overcoming the conflicts which such a fixation always raises, and show no greater evidence of pathology in his career than is seen in the usual saying that "genius is always a little queer." The typical crowd-leader would, on analysis, I think, show something of this "narcissus complex," as would doubtless the great run of fanatics, bigots, and doctrinaires, "hundred per cent" crowd-men all.

According to Brill, these "auto erotic" persons are always homosexual, their homosexuality manifesting itself in various ways. The overt manifestations of this tendency are known as perversions. Certain persons who have suppressed or sublimated these tendencies, by means of certain defense mechanisms, or "fictions," as Adler would call them, get along very well so long as the defense mechanism functions. There are cases when this unconsciously constructed defense breaks down. An inner conflict is then precipitated, a marked form of which is the common type of insanity, "paranoia." Persons suffering with paranoia are characterized by an insatiable demand for love along with a psychic incapacity to give love. They have an exaggerated sense of their own importance which is sustained by a wholly unreal but deadly logical system of *a priori* ideas, which constitute the "obsessions" common to this type of mentality. The inner conflict becomes external—that is, it is "projected." The paranoiac projects his own inner hostility and lack of adjustment upon others—that is, he attributes his own feeling of hostility to some one else, as if he were the object, not the author, of his hatred. He imagines that he is persecuted, as the following example will show. The passage here quoted is taken from a pamphlet which was several years ago given to me by the author. He ostensibly wished to enlist my efforts in a campaign he believed himself to be conducting to "expose" the atrocious treatment of persons, like himself, who were imprisoned in asylums as the innocent victims of domestic conspiracy. By way of introducing himself the author makes it known that he has several times been confined in various hospitals, each time by the design and instigation of his wife, and after stating that on the occasion described he was very "nervous and physically exhausted" and incidentally confessing that he was arrested while attempting homicide "purely in self-defense," he gives this account of his incarceration:

I was locked in a cold cell, and being in poor health, my circulation was poor, and the officer ordered me to go to bed and I obeyed his orders, but I began to get cold, and believing then, as I still believe, that the coffee

I got out of the coffee tank for my midnight lunch had been "doped," and fearful that the blood in my veins which began to coagulate would stop circulating altogether, I got out of bed and walked the floor to and fro all the remainder of the night and by so doing I saved my life. For had I remained in bed two hours I would have been a dead man before sunrise next morning. I realized my condition and had the presence of mind to do everything in my power to save my life and put my trust in God, and asked his aid in my extremity. But for divine aid, I would not now have the privilege of writing my awful experiences in that hell-hole of a jail.

The officer who arrested me without any warrant of law, and without any unlawful act on my part was the tool of some person or persons who were either paid for their heinous crime, or of the landlady of the ——— hotel (he had been a clerk there) who allowed gambling to go on nearly every night, and thought I was a detective or spy, and so was instrumental in having me thrown into jail.

I begged so hard not to be locked in the cell that I was allowed to stay in the corridor in front of the cells. I observed chloral dripping through the roof of the cell-house in different places, and as I had had some experience with different drugs, I detected the smell of chloral as soon as I entered the cell-house.

Sometime after midnight some one stopped up the stovepipe and the door of the coal stove was left open so that the coal gas issued from the stove, so that breathing was difficult in the jail. The gases from the stove and other gases poisoned the air . . . and your humble servant had the presence of mind to tear up a hair mattress and kept my nostrils continually filled with padding out of the mattress. I would often and instantly change the filling in one nostril, and not during the long hours of that awful night did I once open my mouth. In that manner I inhaled very little gases. Why in my weakened condition and my poor health anyone wanted to deprive me of my life I am at a loss to know, but failing to kill me, I was taken after nearly three days of sojourn in that hell-hole to the courthouse in ———. But such thoughts as an innocent man in my condition would think, in among criminals of all sorts, can better be imagined than described. . . . I thought of Christ's persecutors and I thought how the innocent suffer because of the wicked.

In general we may say that the various forms of psychoneurosis are characterized by a conflict of the ego with primitive impulses inadequately repressed. In defense against these impulses, which though active remain unconsciously so, the individual constructs a fictitious system of ideas, of symbolic acts, or bodily symptoms. These systems are attempts to compromise the conflict in the unconscious, and in just the degree that they are demanded for this function, they fail of their function of adjusting the individual to his external world. Thought and behavior thus serve the purpose of compensating for some psychic loss, and of keeping up the individual's self feeling. Though the unconscious purpose is to enhance the ego consciousness, the mechanisms through which this end is achieved produce through their automatic and stereotyped form a shrinking of personality and a serious lack of adjustment to environment.

70

Now it is not at all the aim of this argument to try to prove that crowds are really insane. Psychoanalysts commonly assert that the difference between the normal and the abnormal is largely one of degree and of success in adjustment. We are told that the conflict exists also in normal people, with whom, however, it is adequately repressed and "sublimated"—that is, normal people pass on out of the stages in which the libido of the neurotic becomes fixed, not by leaving them behind, but by attaching the interests which emerge in such stages to ends which are useful in future experience. The neurotic takes the solitary path of resolving the conflict between his ego and the impulses which society demands shall be repressed.

It is altogether conceivable that *another path lies open—that of occasional compromise in our mutual demands on one another*. The force of repression is then relaxed by an unconscious change in the significance of social ideas. Such a change must of course be mutual and unconscious. Compromise mechanisms will again be formed serving a purpose similar to the neurosis. As in the neurosis, thought and action will be compulsory, symbolic, stereotyped, and more or less in conflict with the demands of society as a whole, though functioning in a part of it for certain purposes. Many of the characteristics of the unconscious will then appear and will be similar in some respects to those of neurosis. It is my contention that this is what happens in the crowd, and I will now point out certain phases of crowd-behavior which are strikingly analogous to some of the phenomena which have been described above.

IV

THE EGOISM OF THE CROWD-MIND

THE unconscious egoism of the individual in the crowd appears in all forms of crowd-behavior. As in dreams and in the neurosis this self feeling is frequently though thinly disguised, and I am of the opinion that with the crowd the mechanisms of this disguise are less subtle. To use a term which Freud employs in this connection to describe the process of distortion in dreams, the "censor" is less active in the crowd than in most phases of mental life. Though the conscious thinking is carried on in abstract and impersonal formula, and though, as in the neurosis, the "compulsive" character of the mechanisms developed frequently—especially in permanent crowds—well nigh reduces the individual to an automaton, the crowd is one of the most naïve devices that can be employed for enhancing one's ego consciousness. The individual has only to transfer his repressed self feeling to the idea of the crowd or group of which he is a member; he can then exalt and exhibit himself to almost any extent without shame, oblivious of the fact that the supremacy, power, praise, and glory which he claims for his crowd are really claimed for himself.

That the crowd always insists on being flattered is a fact known intuitively by every orator and editor. As a member of a crowd the individual becomes part of a public. The worship with which men regard "The Public," simply means that the personal self falls at the feet of the same self regarded as public, and likewise demands that obeisance from all. *Vox populi est vox Dei* is obviously the apotheosis of one's own voice while speaking as crowd-man. When this "god-almightiness" manifests itself along the solitary path of the psychoneurosis it becomes one of the common symptoms of paranoia. The crowd, in common with paranoia, uniformly shows this quality of "megalomania." Every crowd "boosts for" itself, lauds itself, gives itself airs, speaks with oracular finality, regards itself as morally superior, and will, so far as it has the power, lord it over everyone. Notice how each group and section in society, so far as it permits itself to think as crowd, claims to be "the people." To the working-class agitator, "the cause of labor is the cause of humanity," workers are always, "innocent exploited victims, kept down by the master

class whose lust for gain has made them
enemies of Humanity and Justice." "Workers should rule because they are the only
useful people; the sole creators of wealth;
their dominance would mean the end of social
wrong, and the coming of the millennium of
peace and brotherhood, the Kingdom of
Heaven on the Earth, the final triumph of
Humanity!"

On the other hand, the wealthy and educated classes speak of themselves as "the
best people"; they *are* "society." It is they
who "bear the burdens of civilization, and
maintain Law and Order and Decency."
Racial and national crowds show the same
megalomania. Hebrews are "God's chosen."
"The Dutch Company is the best Company
that ever came over from the Old Country."
"The Irish may be ornery, and they ain't
worth much, but they are a whole lot better
than the —— —— Dutch." "Little Nigger
baby, black face, and shiny eye, you're just as
good as the poor white trash, an' you'll git thar
by and by." "He might have been a Russian
or a Prussian, . . . but it's greatly to his credit
that he is an Englishman." The German is
the happy bearer of *Kultur* to a barbarian
world. America is "The land of the free
and the home of the brave," and so on, wherever a group has become sufficiently a crowd
to have a propaganda of its own. Presby-

terians are "the Elect," the Catholics have the "true church of God," the Christian Scientists have alone attained "Absolute Truth."

A number of years ago, when the interest in the psychology of the crowd led me to attempt a study of Mr. Sunday's revival meetings, then in their earlier stages, certain facts struck me with great force. Whatever else the revival may be, it provides the student of psychology with a delightful specimen for analysis. Every element of the mob or crowd-mind is present and the unconscious manifests itself with an easy naïveté which is probably found nowhere else, not even in the psychiatric clinic. One striking fact, which has since provided me with food for a good deal of reflection, was the place which the revival holds in what I should like to call the spiritual economy of modern democracy.

It is an interesting historical fact that each great religious revival, from Savonarola down, has immediately followed—and has been the resistance of the man in the street to—a period of intellectual awakening. Mr. Sunday's meetings undeniably provided a device whereby a certain psychic type, an element which had hitherto received scant recognition in the community, could enormously enhance his ego consciousness. It would be manifestly unfair to say that this is the sole motive of the religious revival, or that only this type of mind is active in it. But it is interesting to see whose social survival values stand out most prominently in these religious crowd-phenomena. The gambler, the drunkard, the loafer, the weak, ignorant, and unsuccessful, whose self-esteem it may be assumed had always been made to suffer in small communities, where everyone knew everyone else, had only to yield himself to the pull of the obviously worked-up mechanism of the religious crowd, and lo! all was changed. He was now the repentant sinner, the new convert, over whom there was more rejoicing in heaven, and, what was more visible, also for a brief time, in the Church, than over the ninety and nine just persons. He was "redeemed," an object now of divine love, a fact which anyone who has studied the effects of these crowd-movements scientifically will agree was at once seized upon by these converts to make their own moral dilemmas the standards of righteousness in the community, and hence secure some measure of dominance.

This self-adulation of crowds, with its accompanying will to be important, to dominate, is so constant and characteristic a feature of the crowd-mind that I doubt if any crowd can long survive which fails to perform this function for its members. Self-flattery is evident in the pride with which many people wear badges and other insignia of groups and organizations to which they belong, and in the pompous names by which fraternal orders are commonly designated. In its more "exhibitionist" types it appears in parades and in the favorite ways in which students display their "college spirit." How many school and college "yells" begin with the formula, "Who are We?" obviously designed to call general attention to the group and impress upon people its importance.

In this connection I recall my own student days, which are doubtless typical—the pranks which served the purpose of bringing certain groups of students into temporary prominence and permitted them for a brief period to regard themselves as comic heroes, the practices by which the different classes and societies sought to get the better of one another, the "love feasts" of my society which were hardly more than mutual admiration gatherings, the "pajama" parades in which the entire student body would march in costume (the wearing of which by an isolated individual would probably have brought him before a lunacy commission) all through the town and round and round the dormitories of the women's college a mile or so away, in order to announce a victory in some intercollegiate contest or other. There was the brazenness —it seems hardly credible now—with which the victors on such occasions would permit

themselves to be carried on their comrades'
shoulders through the public square, also the
deportment with which a delegation of students would announce their arrival in a neighboring college town and the grinning self-
congratulation with which we would sit in
chapel and hear a wrathful president denounce our group behavior as "boorishness
and hoodlumism." There was the unanimous conviction of us all, for no other reason
I imagine than that it was graced with our
particular presence, that our own institution
was the most superior college in existence, and
I well remember the priggishness with which
at student banquets we applauded the sentiment repeated *ad nauseam*, that the great aim
of education and the highest mark of excellence in our college was the development of
character. What is it all but a slightly exaggerated account of the egoism of all organized
crowds? Persons of student age are for the
most part still in the normal "narcissus"
period, and their ego-mania is naturally less
disguised than that of older groups. But
even then we could never have given such
open manifestation to it as isolated individuals; it required the crowd-spirit.

The egoism of the crowd commonly takes
the form of the will to social dominance and
it is in crowd behavior that we learn how
insatiable the repressed egoism of mankind

really is. Members of the crowd are always promising one another a splendid future triumph of some sort. This promise of victory, which is nearly always to be enjoyed at the expense, discomfiture, and humiliation of somebody else, is of great advantage in the work of propaganda. People have only to be persuaded that prohibition, or equal suffrage, or the single tax "is coming," and thousands whose reason could not be moved by argument, however logical it might be, will begin to look upon it with favor. The crowd is never so much at home as "on the band wagon." Each of the old political parties gains strength through the repeated prediction of victory in the presidential campaign of 1920. The Socialist finds warmth in the contemplation of the "coming dictatorship of the proletariat." The Prohibitionist intoxicates himself by looking forward to a "dry world." So long as the German crowds expected a victorious end of the war, their morale remained unbroken, the Kaiser was popular.

When a crowd is defeated and its hope of victory fades, the individual soon abandons the unsuccessful group. The great cause, being now a forlorn hope, is seen in a different light, and the crowd character of the group vanishes. When, however, certain forces still operate to keep the crowd state of mind alive—forces such as race feeling, patriotism, religious belief, or class consciousness—the ego consciousness of the individuals so grouped finds escape in the promise of heaven, the Judgment Day, and that "far off divine event toward which the whole creation moves." Meanwhile the hope of victory is changed into that "impotent resentment" so graphically described by Nietzsche.

Another way in which the self feeling of the crowd functions is in idealizing those who succeed in gaining its recognition. The crowd always makes a hero of the public person, living or dead. Regardless of what he really did or was, he is transformed into a symbol of what the crowd wishes to believe him to be. Certain aspects of his teaching and various incidents which would appear in his biography are glossed over, and made into supports for existing crowd-ideas and prejudices. Most of the great characters in history have suffered in this way at the hands of tradition. The secret of their greatness, their uniqueness and spiritual isolation, is in great part ignored. The crowd's own secret is substituted. The great man now appears great because he possessed the qualities of little men. He is representative man, crowd man. Every crowd has a list of heroic names which it uses in its propaganda and in its self-laudation. The greatness which each crowd reveres and demands that all men honor is just that greatness which the crowd treasures as a symbol of itself, the sort of superiority which the members of the crowd may suck up to swell their own ego consciousness.

Thus, hero worship is unconsciously worship of the crowd itself, and the constituents thereof. The self-feeling of a crowd is always enhanced by the triumph of its leader or representative. Who, at a ball game or athletic event, has not experienced elation and added self-complacency in seeing the home team win? What other meaning has the excited cheering? Even a horse on a race track may become the representative of a crowd and lift five thousand people into the wildest joy and ecstasy by passing under a wire a few inches ahead of a rival. We have here one of the secrets of the appeal which all such exhibitions make to people. Nothing so easily catches general attention and creates a crowd as a contest of any kind. The crowd unconsciously identifies its members with one or the other competitor. Success enables the winning crowd to "crow over" the losers. Such an occasion becomes symbolic and is utilized by the ego to enhance its feeling of importance.

A similar psychological fact may be observed in the "jollifications" of political parties after the election of their candidates for high office. This phenomenon is also seen, if I may say so without being misunderstood, in the new spirit which characterizes a people victorious in war, and is to no small degree the basis of the honor of successful nations. It is seen again in the pride which the citizens of a small town show in the fact that the governor of the state is a native of the place. This same principle finds place in such teachings of the Church as the doctrine of the "communion of the saints," according to which the spiritual grace and superiority of the great and pure become the common property of the Church, and may be shared by all believers as a saving grace.

Every organized crowd is jealous of its dignity and honor and is bent upon keeping up appearances. Nothing is more fatal to it than a successful assault upon its prestige. Every crowd, even the casual street mob, clothes the egoistic desires of its members or participants in terms of the loftiest moral motive. No crowd can afford to be laughed at. Crowd men have little sense of humor, certainly none concerning themselves and their crowd-ideas. Any laughter they indulge in is more likely to be directed at those who do not believe with them. The crowd-man resents any suspicion of irreverence or criticism of his professions, because to question them is to weaken the claim of his crowd upon the people, and to destroy in those professed ideals their function of directing his own attention away from the successful compromise of his unconscious conflicts which the crowd had enabled him to make. The crowd would perish if it lost its "ideals." It clings to its fixed ideas with the same tenacity as does the paranoiac. You can no more reason with the former than you can with the latter, and for much the same cause; the beliefs of both are not the fruit of inquiry, neither do they perform the normal intellectual function of adjustment to environment; they are mechanisms of the ego by which it keeps itself in countenance.

Much of the activity of the unconscious ego is viewed by psychologists as "compensation." Devices which serve the purpose of compensating the ego for some loss, act of self-sacrifice, or failure, are commonly revealed by both the normal and the unadjusted. The popular notion that unsatisfied desires sooner or later perish of starvation is at best but a half truth. These desires after we have ceased to attend them become transformed. They frequently find satiety in some substitute which the unconscious accepts as a symbol of its real object. Dreams of normal people contain a great deal of material of this sort. So do day-dreams, and art. Many religious beliefs also serve this purpose of compensation. Jung follows Freud in pointing out as a classic example of the compensation in dreams, that of Nebuchadnezzar, in the Bible.

Nebuchadnezzar at the height of his power had a dream which foretold his downfall. He dreamed of a tree which had raised its head even up to Heaven and now must be hewn down. This was a dream which is obviously a counterpoise to the exaggerated feeling of royal power.

According to Jung, we may expect to find only those things contained in the unconscious which we have not found in the conscious mind. Many conscious virtues and traits of character are thus compensations for their opposite in the unconscious.

In the case of abnormal people, the individual entirely fails to recognize the compensating influences which arise in the unconscious. He even continues to accentuate his onesidedness; this is in accord with the well-known psychological fact that the worst enemy of the wolf is the wolfhound, the greatest despiser of the negro is the mulatto, and that the biggest fanatic is the convert; for I should be a fanatic were I to attack a thing outwardly which inwardly I am obliged to concede is right.

The mentally unbalanced man tries to defend himself against his own unconscious—that is to say, he battles against his own compensating influences. In normal minds opposites of feeling and valuations lie closely associated; the law of this association is called "ambivalence," about which we shall see more later. In the abnormal, the pairs are torn asunder, the resulting division, or strife, leads to disaster, for the unconscious soon begins to intrude itself violently upon the conscious processes.

An especially typical form of unconscious compensation . . . is the paranoia of the alcoholic. The alcoholic loses his love for his wife; the unconscious compensation tries to lead him back again to his duty, but only partially succeeds, for it causes him to become jealous of his wife as if he still loved her. As we know, he may go so far as to kill both his wife and himself, merely out of jealousy. In other words, his love for his wife has not been entirely lost. It has simply become subliminal; but from the realm of consciousness it can now only reappear in the form of jealousy. . . . We see something of a similar nature in the case of the religious convert. . . . The new convert feels himself constrained to defend the faith he has adopted (since much of the old faith still survives in the unconscious associations) in a more or less fanatical way. It is exactly the same in the paranoiac who feels himself constantly constrained to defend himself against all external criticism, because his delusional system is too much threatened from within.

It is not necessary for us to enter here upon a discussion of the processes by which these compensating devices are wrought out in the psychoneurosis. It is significant, though, that Jung calls attention to the likeness between religious fanaticism and paranoia. Now it is obvious that the fanaticism of the religious convert differs psychologically not at all from that of any other convert. We have already noted the fact that most religious conversions are accomplished by the crowd. Moreover

the crowd everywhere tends to fanaticism.
The fanatic is the crowd-man pure and simple.
He is the type which it ever strives to produce.
His excess of devotion, and willingness to
sacrifice both himself and everyone else for
the crowd's cause, always wins the admiration of his fellow crowd-members. He has
given all for the crowd, is wholly swallowed
by it, is "determined not to know anything
save" his crowd and its propaganda. He is
the martyr, the true believer, "the red-blooded
loyal American" with "my country right or
wrong." He is the uncompromising radical
whose prison record puts to shame the less
enthusiastic members of his group. He is the
militant pacifist, the ever-watchful prohibitionist, and keeper of his neighbors' con-
sciences, the belligerent moral purist, who
is scandalized even at the display of lingerie
in the store windows, the professional reformer who in every community succeeds
in making his goodness both indispensable
and unendurable.

One need not be a psychologist to suspect
that the evil against which the fanatic struggles is really in large measure in himself.
He has simply externalized, or "projected"
the conflict in his own unconscious. Persons
who cry aloud with horror at every change in
the style of women's clothing are in most
cases persons whose ego is gnawed by a secret

promiscuous eroticism. The scandalmonger, inhibited from doing the forbidden thing, enjoys himself by a vicarious indulgence in rottenness. The prohibition agitator, if not himself an alcoholic barely snatched from the burning, is likely to be one who at least feels safer in a democracy where it is not necessary to resist temptation while passing a saloon door. Notice that the fanatic or crowd-man always strives to universalize his own moral dilemmas. This is the device by which every crowd seeks dominance in the earth. A crowd's virtues and its vices are really made out of the same stuff. Each is simply the other turned upside down, the compensation for the other. They are alike and must be understood together as the expression of the type of person who constitutes the membership of some particular group or crowd.

I'll never use tobacco, it is a filthy weed
I'll never put it in my mouth, said little Robert Reed.

But obviously, little Robert is already obsessed with a curious interest in tobacco. His first word shows that he has already begun to think of this weed in connection with himself. Should a crowd of persons struggling with Robert's temptation succeed in dominating society, tobacco would become taboo and thus would acquire a moral significance which it does not have at present. So with all our crowd-ethics. The forbidden thing protrudes itself upon consciousness as a negation. The negation reveals what it is that is occupying the inner psyche, and is its compensation. There are certain psychoneuroses in which this negative form of compensation is very marked. Now it is a noteworthy fact that with the crowd the ethical interest always takes this negative form.

The healthy moral will is characterized by a constant restating of the problem of living in terms of richer and higher and more significant dilemmas as new possibilities of personal worth are revealed by experience. New and more daring valuations are constantly made. The whole psychic functioning is enriched. Goodness means an increase of satisfactions through a more adequate adjustment to the real—richer experience, more subtle power of appreciation and command, a self-mastery, sureness, and general personal excellence—which on occasions great and small mark the good will as a reality which counts in the sum total of things. Something is achieved because it is really desired; existence is in so far humanized, a self has been realized. As Professor Dewey says:

If our study has shown anything it is that the moral *is* a life, not something ready-made and complete once for all. It is instinct with movement and struggle, and it is precisely the new and serious situations which call out new vigor and lift it to higher levels.

It is not so with the crowd-ethic. It is interesting to note that from the "Decalogue" to Kant's "Categorical Imperative," crowd-morals always and everywhere take the form of prohibitions, taboos, and ready-made standards, chiefly negative. Freud has made an analytical study of the Taboo as found in primitive society and has shown that it has a compensatory value similar to that of the taboos and compulsions of certain neurotics.

The crowd admits of no personal superiority other than that which consists in absolute conformity to its own negative standards. Except for the valuations expressed by its own dilemmas, "one man is as good as another"—an idea which it can be easily seen serves the purpose of compensation. The goodness which consists of unique personal superiority is very distasteful to the crowd. There must be only one standard of behavior, alike for all. A categorical imperative. The standard as set up is of the sort which is most congenial, possible of attainment, and even necessary for the survival of the members of some particular crowd. It is *their* good, the converse and compensation of their own vices, temptations, and failures. The crowd then demands that this good shall be THE GOOD, that it become the universal standard. By such means even the most incompetent and unadventurous and timid spirits may pass judgment upon all men. They may cry to the great of the earth, "We have piped unto you and you have not danced." Judged by the measure of their conformity to the standards of the small, the great may be considered no better, possibly not so good as the little spirits. The well are forced to behave like the spiritually sick. The crowd is a dog in the manger. If eating meat maketh my brother to be scandalized, or giveth him the cramps, I shall remain a vegetarian so long as the world standeth. Nietzsche was correct on this point. The crowd—he called it the herd —is a weapon of revenge in the hands of the weaker brother. It is a Procrustean bed on which every spiritual superiority may be lopped off to the common measure, and every little ego consciousness may be stretched to the stature of full manhood.

V

THE CROWD A CREATURE OF HATE

PROBABLY the most telling point of likeness between the crowd-mind and the
psychoneurosis—paranoia especially—is the
"delusion of persecution." In cases of paranoia the notion that the patient is the victim
of all sorts of intrigue and persecution is so
common as to be a distinguishing symptom of
this disease. Such delusions are known to
be defenses, or compensation mechanisms,
growing out of the patient's exaggerated feeling of self-importance. The delusion of grandeur and that of being persecuted commonly
go together. The reader will recall the passage quoted from the pamphlet given me by a
typical paranoiac. The author of the docu-
ment mentioned feels that he has a great mission, that of exposing and reforming the conditions in hospitals for the insane. He protests his innocence. In jail he feels like Christ
among his tormentors. His wife has con-
spired against him. The woman who owns
the hotel where he was employed wishes to

put him out of the way. The most fiendish methods are resorted to in order to end his life. "Some one" blocked up the stovepipe, etc., etc.

.Another illustration of a typical case is given by Doctor Brill. I quote scattered passages from the published notes on the case record of the patient, "E. R."

He graduated in 1898 and then took up schoolteaching. . . . He did not seem to get along well with his principal and other teachers. . . . He imagined that the principal and other teachers were trying to work up a "badger game" on him, to the effect that he had some immoral relations with his girl pupils. . . .

In 1903 he married, after a brief courtship, and soon thereafter took a strong dislike to his brother-in-law and sister and accused them of immorality. . . . He also accused his wife of illicit relations with his brother and his brother-in-law, Mr. S.

Mr. S., his brother-in-law, was the arch conspirator against him. He also (while in the hospital) imagined that some women made signs to him and were in the hospital for the purpose of liberating him. Whenever he heard anybody talking he immediately referred it to himself. He interpreted every movement and expression as having some special meaning for himself. . . .

Now and then (after his first release by order of the court) he would send mysterious letters to different persons in New York City. At that time one of his delusions was that he was a great statesman and that the United States government had appointed him ambassador (to Canada), but that the "gang" in New York City had some one without ability to impersonate him so that he lost his appointment. (Later, while confined to the hospital again) he thought that the daughter of the President of the United States came to visit him. . . .

After the patient was recommitted to Bellevue Hospital, he told me that I (Doctor Brill) was one of the "gang." I was no longer his wife in disguise (as he has previously imagined) but his enemy.

Brill's discussion of this case contains an interesting analysis of the several stages of "regression" and the unconscious mechanisms which characterize paranoia. He holds that such cases show a "fixation" in an earlier stage of psychosexual development. The patient, an unconscious homosexual, is really in love with himself. The resulting inner conflict appears, with its defense formations, as the delusion of grandeur and as conscious hatred for the person or persons who happen to be the object of the patient's homosexual wish fancy." However this may be, the point of interest for our study is the "projection" of this hatred to others. Says Brill:

The sentence, "I rather hate him" becomes transformed through projection into the sentence, "he hates (persecutes) me, which justifies my hating him."

The paranoiac's delusional system inevitably brings him in conflict with his environment, but his feeling of being persecuted is less the result of this conflict with an external situation than of his own inner conflict. He convinces himself that it is the other, or others, not he, who is the author of this hatred. He is the innocent victim of their malice.

This phenomenon of "projection and displacement" has received considerable attention in analytical psychology. Freud, in the book, *Totem and Taboo*, shows the role which projection plays in the primitive man's fear of demons. The demons are of course the spirits of the dead. But how comes it that primitive people fear these spirits, and attribute to them every sort of evil design against the living? To quote Freud:

When a wife loses her husband, or a daughter her mother, it not infrequently happens that the survivor is afflicted with tormenting scruples, called "obsessive reproaches," which raise the question whether she herself has not been guilty, through carelessness or neglect, of the death of the beloved person. No recalling of the care with which she nursed the invalid, or direct refutation of the asserted guilt, can put an end to the torture, which is the pathological expression of mourning and which in time slowly subsides. Psychoanalytic investigation of such cases has made us acquainted with the secret mainspring of this affliction. We have ascertained that these obsessive reproaches are in a certain sense justified. . . . Not that the mourner has really been guilty of the death or that she has really been careless, as the obsessive reproach asserts; but still there was something in her, a wish of which she was unaware, which was not displeased with the fact that death came, and which would have brought it about sooner had it been strong enough. The reproach now reacts against this unconscious wish after the death of the beloved person. Such hostility, hidden in the unconscious behind tender love, exists in almost all cases of intensive emotional allegiance to a particular person; indeed, it represents the classic case, the prototype of the ambivalence of human emotions. . . .

By assuming a similar high degree of ambivalence in the emotional life of primitive races such as psychoanalysis ascribes to persons suffering from compulsion neurosis, it becomes comprehensible that the same kind of reaction against the hostility latent in the unconscious behind the obsessive reproaches of the neurotic should also be necessary here after the painful loss has occurred. But this hostility, which is painfully felt in the unconscious in the form of satisfaction with the demise, experiences a different fate in the case of primitive man: the defense against it is accomplished by a displacement upon the object of hostility—namely, the dead. We call this defense process, frequent in both normal and diseased psychic life, a "projection." . . . Thus we find that taboo has grown out of the soil of an ambivalent emotional attitude. The taboo of the dead also originates from the opposition between conscious grief and the unconscious satisfaction at death. If this is the origin of the resentment of spirits, it is self-evident that the nearest and formerly most beloved survivors have to feel it most. As in neurotic symptoms, the taboo regulations evince opposite feelings. Their restrictive character expresses mourning, while they also betray very clearly what they are trying to conceal—namely, the hostility toward the dead which is now motivated as self-defense. . . .

The double feeling—tenderness and hostility—against the deceased, which we consider well-founded, endeavors to assert itself at the time of bereavement as mourning and satisfaction. A conflict must ensue

between these contrary feelings, and as one of them—
namely, the hostility, is altogether, or for the greater
part, unconscious, the conflict cannot result in a conscious difference in the form of hostility or tenderness, as,
for instance, when we forgive an injury inflicted upon
us by some one we love. The process usually adjusts
itself through a special psychic mechanism which is
designated in psychoanalysis as "projection." This
unknown hostility, of which we are ignorant and of
which we do not wish to know, is projected from our
inner perception into the outer world and is thereby
detached from our own person and attributed to
another. Not we, the survivors, rejoice because we are
rid of the deceased, on the contrary we mourn for him;
but now, curiously enough, he has become an evil
demon who would rejoice in our misfortune and who
seeks our death. The survivors must now defend
themselves against this evil enemy; they are freed
from inner oppression, but they have only succeeded
in exchanging it for an affliction from without.

Totem, taboo, demon worship, etc., are
clearly primitive crowd-phenomena. Freud's
main argument in this book consists in showing
the likeness between these phenomena and the
compulsion neurosis. The projection of unconscious hostility upon demons is by no
means the only sort of which crowds both
primitive and modern are capable. Neither
must the hostility always be unconscious.
Projection is a common device whereby even
normal and isolated individuals justify themselves in hating. Most of us love to think
evil of our enemies and opponents. Just as

two fighting schoolboys will each declare that the other "began it," so our dislike of people often first appears to our consciousness as a conviction that they dislike or entertain unfriendly designs upon us. There is a common type of female neurotic whose repressed erotic wishes appear in the form of repeated accusations that various of her men acquaintances are guilty of making improper advances to her. When the "white slavery" reform movement swept over the country—an awakening of the public conscience which would have accomplished a more unmixed good if it had not been taken up in the usual crowd-spirit—it was interesting to watch the newspapers and sensational propagandist speakers as they deliberately encouraged these pathological phenomena in young people. The close psychological relation between the neurosis and the crowd-mind is shown by the fact that the two so frequently appear at the same moment, play so easily into each other's hands, and are apparently reactions to the very same social situation.

In Brill's example of paranoia, it will be remembered that the patient's delusions of persecution took the form of such statements as that the "gang" had intrigued at Washington to prevent his appointment as ambassador, that certain of his relatives were in a "conspiracy against him." How commonly such phrases and ideas occur in crowd-oratory and in the crowd-newspaper is well known to all. We have already seen that the crowd in most cases identifies itself with "the people," "humanity," "society," etc. Listen to the crowd-orator and you will also learn that there are all sorts of abominable "conspiracies" against "the people." "The nation is full of traitors." The Church is being "undermined by cunning heretics." "The Bolshevists are in secret league with the Germans to destroy civilization." "Socialists are planning to corrupt the morals of our youth and undermine the sacredness of the home." "The politicians' gang intends to loot the community." "Wall Street is conspiring to rob the people of their liberties." "England plans to reduce America to a British colony again." "Japan is getting ready to make war on us." "German merchants are conducting a secret propaganda intending to steal our trade and pauperize our nation." "The Catholics are about to seize power and deliver us over to another Inquisition." "The liquor interests want only to make drunkards of our sons and prostitutes of our daughters." And so on and so forth, wherever any crowd can get a hearing for its propaganda. Always the public welfare is at stake; society is threatened. The "wrongs" inflicted upon an innocent humanity are rehearsed. Bandages are taken off every social wound. Every scar, be it as old as Cromwell's mistreatment of Ireland, is inflamed. "The people are being deceived," "kept down," "betrayed." They must rise and throw off their exploiters, or they must purge the nation of disloyalty and "anarchy."

It cannot be denied that our present social order is characterized by deep and fundamental social injustices, nor that bitter struggles between the various groups in society are inevitable. But the crowd forever ignores its own share in the responsibility for human ills, and each crowd persists in making a caricature of its enemies, real and imagined, nourishing itself in a delusion of persecution which is like nothing so much as the characteristic obsessions of the paranoiac. This suspiciousness, this habit of misrepresentation and exaggeration of every conceivable wrong, is not only a great hindrance to the conflicting groups in adjusting their differences, it makes impossible, by misrepresenting the real issue at stake, any effective struggle for ideals. As the history of all crowd movements bears witness, the real source of conflict is forgotten, the issue becomes confused with the spectacular, the unimportant, and imagnary. Energy is wasted on side issues, and the settlement finally reached, even by a clearly victorious crowd, is seldom that of the original matter in dispute. In fact, it is not at all the function of these crowd-ideas of self-pity and persecution to deal with real external situations. These ideas are propaganda. Their function is to keep the crowd together, to make converts, to serve as a defense for the egoism of the crowd-man, to justify the anticipated tyranny which it is the unconscious desire of the individual to exercise in the moment of victory for his crowd, and, as "they who are not for us are against us," to project the crowd-man's hatred upon the intended victims of his crowd's will to universal dominion. In other words, these propaganda ideas serve much the same end as do the similar delusions of persecution in paranoia.

This likeness between the propaganda of the crowd and the delusions of paranoia is illustrated daily in our newspapers. The following items cut from the New York *Tribune* are typical. The first needs no further discussion, as it parallels the cases given above. The second is from the published proceedings of "a committee," appointed, as I remember it, by the assembly of the state of New York, to conduct an investigation into certain alleged seditious and anarchist activities. These articles well illustrate the character of the propaganda to which such a committee almost inevitably lends itself. Whether the committee or the newspapers were chiefly responsible for such fabrications, I do not know, but the crowd character of much of the attempt to stamp out Bolshevism is strikingly revealed in this instance. No doubt the members of this committee, as well as the detectives and the press agents who are associated with them, are as honestly convinced that a mysterious gang of radicals is planning to murder us all as is the paranoiac W. H. M. fixed in his delusion that his enemies are trying to asphyxiate him. It will be remembered that Brill's patient "E. S." interpreted "every movement and expression as having some special meaning for himself." This kind of "interpretation" has a curious logic all its own. It is what I would call "compulsive thinking," and is characteristic of both the delusions of paranoia and the rumors of the crowd.

First clipping:

INVENTOR IS DECLARED INSANE BY A JURY.

W. H. M. declares rivals are attempting to asphyxiate him. W. H. M., an inventor, was declared mentally incompetent yesterday by a jury in the Sheriff's court. . . . Alienists said M. had hallucinations about enemies who he thinks are trying to asphyxiate him. He also imagines that he is under hypnotic influences and that persons are trying to affect his body with "electrical influences."

Second clipping:

THE CROWD A CREATURE OF HATE

Several hundred men, formerly in United States Service, signify willingness to aid in project. A "Red Guard" composed of men who have served in the American military establishment is contemplated in the elaborate revolutionary plans of Bolshevik leaders here. This was learned yesterday when operatives of the Lusk committee discovered that the radicals were making every effort to enlist the aid of the Soldiers, Sailors, and Marines Protective Association in carrying out a plot to overthrow the government by force. As far as the detectives have been able to ascertain, the great mass of fighting men are not in sympathy with the Reds, but several hundred have signified their willingness to co-operate.

Just how far the plans of the Reds have progressed was not revealed. It is known, however, that at a convention of the Left Wing Socialists in Buffalo the movement designed to enlist the support of the Soldiers, Sailors, and Marines Protective Association was launched. This convention was addressed by prominent Left Wingers from Boston, New York, Philadelphia, Pittsburgh, and Paterson. They asserted that trained military men must be obtained for the organization if the plans were to be successful.

It was from this meeting, which was held in secret, that agitators were sent to various parts of the state to form soviets in the shops and factories. This phase of the radical activity, according to the investigators, has met with considerable success in some large factory districts where most of the workers are foreign-born. In some places the soviets in the shops have become so strong that the employers are alarmed and have notified the authorities of the menace. When sufficient evidence has been gathered, foreign-born agitators working to cause unrest in factories will be apprehended and recommended for deportation.

Later report:

DENIES FORMATION OF "RED GUARD" IN U. S.

Alfred Levitt, secretary of the Soldiers, Sailors, and Marines Protective Association, yesterday emphatically denied that the organization was to be used as a "Red Guard" by the radicals when they started their contemplated revolution. He said he never had heard any of the members of the association discuss the formation of a "Red Guard" but admitted that many of them were radicals.

In the two instances given above, fear, suspicion, hatred, give rise in one case to a delusional system in the mind of an isolated individual, and in the other to the circulation of an unfounded rumor by men who in their right minds would, to say the least, carefully scrutinize the evidence for such a story before permitting it to be published. As several months have passed since the publication of this story and nothing more has appeared which would involve our returned service men in any such treasonable conspiracy, I think it is safe to say that this story, like many others circulated by radicals as well as by reactionaries during the unsettled months following the war, has its origin in the unconscious mechanisms of crowd-minded people.

Every sort of crowd is prone to give credence
to rumors of this nature, and to accuse all
those who can not at once give uncritical
acceptance to such tales of sympathy with the
enemy. Later we shall have something to
say about the delusional systems which appear
to be common to the crowd-mind and the
paranoiac. In this connection I am interested
in pointing out only the psychological relation
between what I might call the "conspiracy
delusion" and unconscious hatred. Commonly the former is the "projection" of the
latter.

One of the differences between these two
forms of "projection" is the fact that the
hatred of the crowd is commonly less "rationalized" than in paranoia—that is, less successfully disguised. Like the paranoiac, every
crowd is potentially if not actually homicidal
in its tendencies. But whereas with the paranoiac the murderous hostility remains for the
greater part an unconscious "wish fancy,"
and it is the mechanisms which disguise it or
serve as a defense against it which appear to
consciousness, with the crowd the murder-
wish will itself appear to consciousness whenever the unconscious can fabricate such defense mechanisms as will provide it with a
fiction of moral justification. Consequently,
it is this fiction of justification which the
crowd-man must defend.

The crowd's delusion of persecution, conspiracy, or oppression is thus a defense mechanism of this nature. The projection of this hatred on those outside the crowd serves not so much, as in paranoia, to shield the subject from the consciousness of his own hatred, as to provide him with a pretext for exercising it. Given such a pretext, most crowds will display their homicidal tendencies quite openly.

Ordinary mobs or riots would seem to need very little justification of this sort. But even these directly homicidal crowds invariably represent themselves as motivated by moral idealism and righteous indignation. Negroes are lynched in order to protect the white womanhood of the South, also because, once accused, the negro happens to be helpless. If the colored people were in the ascendancy and the whites helpless we should doubtless see the reverse of this situation. A community rationally convinced of the culprit's guilt could well afford to trust the safety of womanhood to the justice meted out by the courts, but it is obvious that these "moral" crowds are less interested in seeing that justice is done than in running no risk of losing their victim, once he is in their power. A recent development of this spirit is the lynching in a Southern town of a juror who voted for the acquittal of a black man accused of a crime.

It may be taken as a general law of crowd-psychology that the "morality" of the crowd always demands a victim. Is it likely that one of these mobs would "call off" an interesting lynching party if at the last minute it were demonstrated that the accused was innocent? The practice of lynching has been extended, from those cases where the offense with which the accused is charged is so revolting as justly to arouse extreme indignation, to offenses which are so trivial that they merely serve as a pretext for torture and killing.

The homicidal tendencies of the crowd-mind always reveal themselves the minute the crowd becomes sufficiently developed and powerful to relax for the time being the usual social controls. Illustrations of this may be seen in the rioting between the white and the colored races—epidemics of killing—such as occurred recently in East St. Louis, and in the cities of Washington, Chicago, and Omaha. The same thing is evident in the "pogroms" of Russia and Poland, in the acts of revolutionary mobs of Germany and Russia, in the promptness with which the Turks took advantage of the situation created by the war to slaughter the Armenians. This hatred is the specter which forever haunts the conflict between labor and capital. It is what speedily transformed the French Revolution from the dawn of an era of "Fraternity" to a day of terror and intimidation. It is seen again in the curious interest which the public always has in a sensational murder trial. It is evident in the hostility, open or suppressed, with which any community regards the strange, the foreign, the "outlandish"— an example of which is the frequent bullying and insulting of immigrants in this country since the war. Much of the "Americanization propaganda" which we have carried on since the war unfortunately gave the typical crowd-man his opportunity. One need only listen to the speeches or read the publications of certain "patriotic" societies to learn why it was that the exhortation to our foreign neighbors to be loyal did so much more harm than good.

The classic example of the killing crowd is, of course, a nation at war. There are, to be sure, wars of national self-defense which are due to political necessity rather than to crowd-thinking, but even in such cases the phenomena of the crowd are likely to appear to the detriment of the cause. At such times not only the army but the whole nation becomes a homicidal crowd. The army, at least while the soldiers are in service, probably shows the crowd-spirit in a less degree than does the civilian population. The mental processes of an entire people are transformed. Every interest — profit-seeking excepted — is subordinated to the one passion to crush the enemy. The moment when war is declared is usually hailed with tremendous popular enthusiasm and joy. There is a general lifting of spirits. There is a sense of release, a nation-wide exultation, a sigh of relief as we feel the deadening hand of social control taken from our throats. The homicidal wish-fancy, which in peace times and in less sovereign crowds exists only as an hypothesis, can now become a reality. And though it is doubtful if more than one person in a million can ever give a rational account of just what issue is really at stake in any war, the conviction is practically unanimous that an occasion has been found which justifies, even demands, the release of all the repressed hostility in our natures. The fact that in war time this crowd hostility may, under certain circumstances, really have survival value and be both beneficial and necessary to the nation, is to my mind not a justification of crowd-making. It is rather a revelation of the need of a more competent leadership in world politics.

Unconsciously every national crowd, I mean the crowd-minded element in the nation, carries a chip on its shoulder, and swaggers and challenges its neighbors like a young town-bully on his way home from grammar school. This swaggering, which is here the "compulsive manifestation" of unconscious hos-

tility characteristic of every crowd, appears
to consciousness as "national honor." To
the consciousness of the nation-crowd the
quarrel for which it has been spoiling for a
long time always appears to have been "forced
upon it." Some nations are much more
quarrelsome than others. I cannot believe
that our conviction that Imperial Germany
was the aggressor in the great war is due
merely to patriotic conceit on our part. The
difference between our national spirit and that
of Imperial Prussia is obvious, but the difference in this respect, great as it is, is one of
degree rather than of kind, and is due largely
to the fact that the political organization of
Germany permitted the Prussian patriots to
hold the national mind in a permanent crowd
state to a degree which is even now hardly
possible in this republic. My point is that a
nation becomes warlike to precisely the extent that its people may be made to think and
behave as a crowd. Once a crowd, it is always "in the right" however aggressive and
ruthless its behavior; every act or proposal
which is calculated to involve the nation-
crowd in a controversy, which gains some advantage over neighboring peoples, or intensi-
fies hatred once it is released, is wildly applauded. Any dissent from the opinions of
our particular party or group is trampled
down. He who fails at such a time to be a

crowd-man and our own sort of a crowd-man is a "slacker." Everyone's patriotism is put under suspicion, political heresy-hunting is the rule, any personal advantage which can be gained by denouncing as "enemy sympathizers" rival persons or groups within the nation is sure to be snatched up by some one. The crowd-mind, even in times of peace, distorts patriotism so that it is little more than a compulsive expression and justification of repressed hostility. In war the crowd succeeds in giving rein to this hostility by first projecting it upon the enemy.

Freud in his little book, *War and Death,* regards war as a temporary "regression" in which primitive impulses which are repressed by civilization, but not eradicated, find their escape. He argues that most people live psychologically "beyond their means." Hence war could be regarded, I suppose, as a sort of "spiritual liquidation." But if the hostility which the war crowd permits to escape is simply a repressed impulse to cruelty, we should be obliged to explain a large part of crowd-behavior as "sadistic." This may be the case with crowds of a certain type, lynching mobs, for instance. But as the homicidal tendencies of paranoia are not commonly explained as sadism, I can see no reason why those of the crowd should be. Sadism is a return to an infantile sex perversion, and in its direct overt forms the resulting conflicts are conscious and are between the subject and environment. It is where a tendency unacceptable to consciousness is repressed—and inadequately—that neurotic conflict ensues. This conflict being inner, develops certain mechanisms for the defense of the ego-feeling which is injured. The hatred of the paranoiac is really a defense for his own injured self-feeling. As the crowd always shows an exaggerated ego-feeling similar to the paranoiac's delusion of grandeur, and as in cases of paranoia this inner conflict is always "projected" in the form of delusions of persecution, may we not hold that the characteristic hostility of the crowd is also in some way a device for protecting this inflated self-appreciation from injury? The forms which this hatred takes certainly have all the appearance of being "compulsive" ideas and actions.

We have been discussing crowds in which hostility is present in the form of overt destructive and homicidal acts or other unmistakable expressions of hatred. But are there not also peaceable crowds, crowds devoted to religious and moral propaganda, idealist crowds? Yes, all crowds moralize, all crowds are also idealistic. But the moral enthusiasm of the crowd always demands a victim. The idealist crowd also always makes idols of its ideals and worships them with human sacrifice. The peaceable crowd is only potentially homicidal. The death-wish exists as a fancy only, or is expressed in symbols so as to be more or less unrecognizable to ordinary consciousness. I believe that *every crowd is "against some one."* Almost any crowd will persecute on occasion—if sufficiently powerful and directly challenged. The crowd tends ever to carry its ideas to their deadly logical conclusion.

I have already referred to the crowd's interest in games and athletic events as an innocent symbolization of conflict. How easy it is to change this friendly rivalry into sudden riot—its real meaning—every umpire of baseball and football games knows. As an illustration of my point—namely, that the enthusiasm aroused by athletic contests is the suppressed hostility of the crowd, I give the following. In this letter to a New York newspaper, the writer, a loyal "fan," reveals the same mentality that we find in the sectarian fanatic, or good party man, whose "principles" have been challenged. The challenge seems in all such cases to bring the hostility into consciousness as "righteous indignation."

To the Editor:

Sir,—The article under the caption "Giants' Chances for Flag to be Settled in Week," on the sporting page of the *Tribune*, is doubtless intended to be humorous.

The section referring to the Cincinnati baseball public is somewhat overdrawn, to say the least, and does not leave a very favorable impression on the average Cincinnatian, such as myself. I have been a reader of your paper for some time, but if this sort of thing continues I shall feel very much like discontinuing.

W. L. D.

The extremes to which partisan hatred and jealousy can lead even members of the United States Senate, the intolerance and sectarian spirit which frequently characterize crowds, the "bigotry" of reformist crowds, are matters known to us all. Does anyone doubt that certain members of the Society for the Prevention of Vice, or of the Prohibitionists, would persecute if they had power? Have not pacifist mass meetings been known to break up in a row? The Christian religion is fundamentally a religion of love, but the Church has seldom been wholly free from the crowd-spirit, and the Church crowd will persecute as quickly as any other. In each period of its history when Christian believers have been organized as dominant crowds the Church has resorted to the severest forms of persecution. Popular religion always demands some kind of devil to stand as the permanent object of the believer's hostility. Let an editor, or lecturer, or clergyman anywhere attack some one, and he at once gains following and popularity. Evangelists and political orators are always able to "get" their crowd by resorting to abuse of some one. Let any mass meeting become a crowd, and this note of hostility inevitably appears.

Notice the inscriptions which commonly appear on the banners carried in political or labor parades. On the day after the armistice was signed with Germany, when the most joyous and spontaneous crowds I have ever seen filled the streets of New York, I was greatly impressed with those homemade banners. Though it was the occasion of the most significant and hard-won victory in human history, there was hardly a reference to the fact. Though it was the glad moment of peace for which all had longed, I did not see ten banners bearing the word "Peace," even in the hands of the element in the city who were known to be almost unpatriotically pacifist. But within less than an hour I counted on Fifth Avenue more than a hundred banners bearing the inscription, "To Hell with the Kaiser."

That the man chiefly responsible for the horrors of the war should be the object of universal loathing is only to be expected, but the significant fact is that of all the sentiments which swept into people's minds on that occasion, this and this alone should have been immediately seized upon when the crowd spirit began to appear. I doubt if at the time there

was a very clear sense of the enormity of
Wilhelm's guilt in the minds of those laughing
people. The Kaiser was hardly more than a
symbol. The antagonist, whoever he be, was
"fallen down to hell," our own sense of triumph was magnified by the depth of his fall.
Just so the Hebrew Prophet cried "Babylon
is fallen," so the early Christians pictured
Satan cast into the bottomless pit, so the
Jacobins cried "*A bas les Aristocrats*," our
own Revolutionary crowds cried "Down with
George III," and the Union soldiers sang,
"Hang Jeff Davis on a Sour Apple Tree." I
repeat that wherever the crowd-mind appears,
it will always be found to be "against" some
one.

An interesting fact about the hostility of a
crowd is its ability on occasion to survive the
loss of its object. It may reveal the phenomenon which psychologists call "displacement." That is to say, another object may
be substituted for the original one without
greatly changing the quality of the feeling. A
mob in the street, driven back from the object
of its attack, will loot a store or two before it
disperses. Or, bent on lynching a certain
negro, it may even substitute an innocent
man, if robbed of its intended victim—as, for
instance, the lynching of the mayor of Omaha.
Such facts would seem to show that these
hostile acts are really demanded by mech-

anisms within the psyche. Many symbolic acts of the person afflicted with compulsion neurosis show this same *trait of substitution*. If inhibited in the exercise of one mechanism of escape, the repressed wish will substitute another. Also anyone associated by the unconscious reasoning with the hated object, or anyone who tries to defend him or prove him innocent, may suffer from this crowd's hatred. Freud has analyzed this phenomenon in his study of taboo. He who touches the tabooed object himself becomes taboo.

I have said that the hostility of the crowd is a sort of "defense mechanism." That this is so in certain cases, I think can be easily demonstrated. The following news item is an example of the manner in which such hostility may serve as a "defense mechanism" compensating the self-feeling for certain losses and serving to enhance the feeling of self-importance:

CHARGES BAKER HAD 57 BRANDS OF ARMY OBJECTOR.

———, OF MINNESOTA, DEFENDING MARINES FATHERS' ASSOCIATION PROTEST; ASSAILS FREEING OF "SLACKERS."

WASHINGTON, *July 23*.—A bitter partisan quarrel developed in the House today when Representative ———, of Minnesota, attacked Secretary Baker and the President for the government's policy toward conscientious objectors. The attack was the result of protests

117

by the Marines Fathers' Association of Minneapolis, Minnesota, representing between 500 and 600 young marines now in France, all from the Minneapolis high schools and the University of Minnesota, and many in the famous 6th Regiment of Marines that took a big part in stopping the Germans at Chateau Thierry.

Upon learning of the treatment accorded conscientious objectors in this country while their sons were dying in France, the association asked Representative —— to fix the responsibility for the government's policy. Representative —— fixed it today as that of Secretary Baker and President Wilson, charging that they extended the definition of those to be exempted from military service laid down by Congress in an act of May 17, 1917.

"One variety of conscientious objector was not enough for Mr. Baker," declared Representative ——. "He had 57 kinds. . . . "

Representative ——, of Arizona, defended Secretary Baker, asserting that of 20,000 men who were certified as conscientious objectors, 16,000 ultimately went to war. The case of Sergt. Alvin C. York, the Tennessee hero, who had conscientious objections at first, but soon changed his mind, was cited in defense of the War Department's policy.

Let us pass over the obviously partisan element in this Congressional debate—a crowd phenomenon in itself, by the way—and consider the mental state of this Fathers' Association.

In spite of the fact that the treatment of those who refused military service in this country was so much more severe than the manner with which the British government is reported to have dealt with this class of persons, that many people, including the Secretary of War, whose loyalty except to partisan minds was above suspicion, sought in the name of humanity to alleviate some of the conditions in our military prisons, it was not severe enough to satisfy these "fathers." It is doubtful if anything short of an *auto da fe* would have met their approval. Now no one believes that these simple farmers from the Northwest are such sadists at heart that they enjoy cruelty for its own sake. I imagine that the processes at work here are somewhat as follows:

The telltale phrase here is that these farmers' sons "were dying in France." Patriotic motives rightly demanded that fathers yield their sons to the hardship and danger of battle, and while the sacrifice was made consciously, with willingness and even with pride in having done their painful duty, it was not accomplished without struggle—the unconscious resisted it. It could not be reconciled to so great a demand. In other words, these fathers, and probably many of their sons also, were unconsciously "conscientious objectors." Unconsciously they longed to evade this painful duty, but these longings were put aside, "repressed" as shameful and cowardly—that is, as unacceptable to conscious self-feeling. It was necessary to defend the ego against these longings. Compensation was demanded and found in the nation-wide recognition of the value of this patriotic sacrifice. Expressions of patriotic sentiment on the part of others, therefore, compensated the individual and enhanced his self-feeling.

Successful refusal anywhere to recognize the duty which consciously motivated this sacrifice strengthened the unconscious desire to evade it. The unconscious reasoning was something like this: "If those men got out of this thing, why should not we? Since we had to bear this loss, they must also. We have suffered for duty's sake. By making them suffer also, they will be forced to recognize this 'duty' with which we defend ourselves against our sense of loss and desire to escape it." As a witness to the values against which the ego of these fathers has to struggle, the existence of the conscientious objector, in a less degree of suffering than their own, is as intolerable as their own "shameful and cowardly" unconscious longings. Hostility to the conscientious objector is thus a "projection" of their own inner conflict. By becoming a crowd, the members of this "Fathers' Association" make it mutually possible to represent their hostility to conscientious objectors as something highly patriotic. Secretary Baker's alleged leniency to these hated persons is now not only an affront to these fathers, it is an affront to the entire nation.

Another and somewhat different example of the function of hatred in the service of the self-feeling is the following item, which throws some light on the motives of the race riots in Washington. This is, of course, a defense of but one of the crowds involved, but it is interesting psychologically.

NEGRO EDITOR BLAMES WHITES FOR RACE RIOTS.

Dr. W. F. B. DuBois, of 70 Fifth Avenue, editor of *The Crisis*, a magazine published in connection with the work of the National Association for the Advancement of the Colored People, yesterday attributed the race riots in Washington to the irritability of all people and the unsettling of many ideas caused by the war, to the influx of a large number of Southerners into Washington, and to the *presence in that city of many of the representatives of the educated, well-dressed class of negroes* which white racial antagonists dislike.

Washington policemen are notoriously unfriendly to the colored people, he added. Time and time again they stand by and witness a dispute between a white man and a negro, and when it is over and the negro has been beaten they arrest the negro, and not the white man who caused the trouble in the first place.

The colored editor pointed out the similarity between the present riots in Washington and the Atlanta riots which occurred about twelve years ago. In both places, he said, white hoodlums began rioting and killing negroes. When the latter became aroused and began to retaliate, the authorities stepped in and the rioting stopped.

9   121

Major J. E. Spingarn, acting treasurer of the National Association for the Advancement of the Colored People, said the *soldiers and sailors who have been taking part in the rioting in Washington resent the new attitude of self-respect which the negro has assumed because of the part he played in the war.*

"The soldiers," he said, "instead of fighting the negroes because the latter think better of themselves for having fought in the war, should respect them for having proved themselves such good fighters." (The italics are mine.)

It is quite possible that in most communities where such race riots occur certain members of the colored race are responsible to the extent that they have made themselves conspicuously offensive to their white neighbors.

But such individual cases, even where they exist, do not justify attacks upon hundreds of innocent people. And it must be said that in general the kind of people whose feelings of personal superiority can find no other social support than the mere fact that they happen to belong to the white race—and I think it will be found that the mobs who attack negroes are uniformly made of people who belong to this element—naturally find their self-feeling injured "if a nigger puts on airs." Their fiction is challenged; to accept the challenge would force upon the consciousness of such people a correct estimate of their own worth. Such an idea is unacceptable to consciousness. The presumptuous negroes who serve as such unpleasant reminders "must be put in their proper place"—that is, so completely under the feet of the white element in the community that the mere fact of being a white man may serve as a defense mechanism for just those members of our noble race who approach more closely to the social position of the colored element in our midst.

As the moral standards of the community will not permit even this element of the white race to play the hoodlum with self-approval, some disguise or "displacement" for this motive must be found whereby the acts to which it prompts may appear to the consciousness of their perpetrators as justifiable. A misdeed is committed by a black man; instantly this element of the white race becomes a crowd. The deed provides the whites with just the pretext they want. They may now justify themselves and one another in an assault on the whole colored community. Here I believe we have the explanation of much that is called "race prejudice." The hatred between the races, like all crowd-hatred, is a "defense mechanism" designed to protect the ego in its conflict with ideas unacceptable to consciousness.

The intensest hatred of the crowd is that directed toward the heretic, the nonconformist, the "traitor." I have sometimes thought

that to the crowd-mind there is only one sin,
heresy. Every sort of crowd, political, religious, moral, has an ax ready for the person
who in renouncing its ideas and leaving it
threatens to break it up. The bitter partisan
hatred of crowds is nothing compared to their
hatred for the renegade. To the crowd of
true believers, the heretic or schismatic is
"worse than the infidel." The moral crowd
will "bear with" the worst *roué* if only he
strives to keep up appearances, has a guilty
conscience, asks forgiveness, and professes
firm belief in the conventions against which he
offends; one may be forgiven his inability to
"live up to his principles" if only his professed principles are the same as the crowd's.
But let a Nietzsche, though his life be that of
an ascetic, openly challenge and repudiate
the values of popular morality, and his name
is anathema.

As an example of the hatred of the political
crowd for one who, having once put his hand
to the plow and turned back, henceforth is no
longer fit for the "kingdom," I quote the
following from an ultraradical paper. It is
hard to believe that this passage was written
by a man who, in his right mind, is really
intelligent and kind-hearted, but such is the
case:

AN EXPLANATION.—Owing to a failure of editorial
supervision we published an advertisement of John

Spargo's book on Bolshevism. We have returned the money we received for it, and canceled the contract for its future appearances. We do not pretend to protect our readers against patent-medicine swindlers, real-estate sharpers, canned goods prevaricators, ptomaine poisoners, fairy bond-sellers, picaroon nickel-pickers, subway ticket speculators, postage-stamp forgers, pie and pancake counterfeiters, plagiary burglars, lecherous pornographers, and pictorial back-porch climbers, plundering buccaneer blackmailers and defaulting matrimonial agents, journalistic poachers, foragers, pickpockets, thimbleriggers, lick-sauce publicity men, notoriety hunters, typographical body-snatchers, blackletter assassins, and promulgators of licentious meters in free verse. Against these natural phenomena we offer no guarantee to our readers, but we never intended to advertise John Spargo's book on Bolshevism.

Here again, it seems, the reason for hatred is "self-defense." One important difference between the crowd-mind and the psychosis is the fact that while the psychic mechanisms of the latter serve to disguise the inadequately repressed wish, those of the crowd-mind permit the escape of the repressed impulse by relaxing the force which demands the repression—namely, the immediate social environment. This relaxation is accomplished by a general fixation of attention which changes for those who share it the moral significance of the social demand. The repressed wish then appears to consciousness in a form which meets with the mutual approval of the individuals so affected. Or, as I have said, the social environment, instead of acting as a check upon the realization of the wish-fancy, slips along in the same direction with it. Hence the will to believe the same, so characteristic of every crowd. As soon as this mutuality is broken the habitual criteria of the real again become operative. Every individual who "comes to" weakens the hold of the crowd-ideas upon all the others to just the extent that his word must be taken into account. The crowd resorts to all sorts of devices to bind its members together permanently in a common faith. It resists disintegration as the worst conceivable evil. Disintegration means that crowd-men must lose their pet fiction—which is to say, their "faith." The whole system elaborated by the unconscious fails to function; its value for compensation, defense, or justification vanishes as in waking out of a dream.

Strong spirits can stand this disillusionment. They have the power to create new, more workable ideals. They become capable of self-analysis. They learn to be legislators of value and to revise their beliefs for themselves. Their faiths become not refuges, but instruments for meeting and mastering the facts of experience and giving them meaning. The strong are capable of making their lives spiritual adventures in a real world. The "truths" of such persons are not compulsive ideas, they are working hypotheses which they are ready, as occasion may demand, to verify at great personal risk, or to discard when proved false. Such persons sustain themselves in their sense of personal worth less by defense mechanisms than by the effort of will which they can make.

As William James said:

If the searching of our heart and reins be the purpose of this human drama, then what is sought seems to be what effort we can make. He who can make none is but a shadow; he who can make much is a hero. The huge world that girdles us about puts all sorts of questions to us, and tests us in all sorts of ways. Some of the tests we meet by actions that are easy, and some of the questions we answer in articulately formulated words. But the deepest question that is ever asked admits of no reply but the dumb turning of the will and tightening of our heartstrings as we say, "Yes, I will even have it so!" When a dreadful object is presented, or when life as a whole turns up its dark abysses to our view, then the worthless ones among us lose their hold on the situation altogether, and either escape from its difficulties by averting their attention, or, if they cannot do that, collapse into yielding masses of plaintiveness and fear. The effort required for facing and consenting to such objects is beyond their power to make. But the heroic mind does differently. To it, too, the objects are sinister and dreadful, unwelcome, incompatible with wished-for things. But it can face them if necessary without losing its hold upon the rest of life. The world thus finds in the heroic man its worthy match and mate. . . . He can *stand* this Universe.

Indeed the path for all who would make of living a reality rather than an imitation leads along what James used to call "the perilous edge." Every personal history that is a history, and not a mere fiction, contains in it something unique, a fraction for which there is no common denominator. It requires just that effort of attention to concrete reality and the fact of self which in the crowd we always seek to escape by diverting attention to congenial abstractions and ready-made universals. We "find ourselves" only as we "get over" one after another of our crowd-compulsions, until finally we are strong enough, as Ibsen would say, "to stand alone."

Timid spirits seldom voluntarily succeed in getting closer to reality than the "philosophy of *'as if'*" which characterizes the thinking both of the crowd and the psychoneurosis. What indeed is the crowd but a fiction of upholding ourselves by all leaning on one another, an "escape from difficulties by averting attention," a spiritual safety-first or "fool-proof" mechanism by which we bear up one another's collapsing ego-consciousness lest it dash its foot against a stone?

The crowd-man can, when his fiction is challenged, save himself from spiritual bankruptcy, preserve his defenses, keep his crowd from going to pieces, only by a demur. Anyone who challenges the crowd's fictions must be ruled out of court. He must not be permitted to speak. As a witness to contrary values his testimony must be discounted. The worth of his evidence must be discredited by belittling the disturbing witness. "He is a bad man; the crowd must not listen to him." His motives must be evil; he "is bought up"; he is an immoral character; he tells lies; he is insincere or he "has not the courage to take a stand" or "there is nothing new in what he says." Ibsen's "Enemy of the People," illustrates this point very well. The crowd votes that Doctor Stockman may not speak about the baths, the real point at issue. Indeed, the mayor takes the floor and officially announces that the doctor's statement that the water is bad is "unreliable and exaggerated." Then the president of the Householder's Association makes an address accusing the doctor of secretly "*aiming at revolution.*" When finally Doctor Stockman speaks and tells his fellow citizens the real meaning of their conduct, and utters a few plain truths about "the compact majority," the crowd saves its face, not by proving the doctor false, but by howling him down, voting him an "enemy of the people," and throwing stones through his windows.

A crowd is like an unsound banking institution. People are induced to carry their deposits of faith in it, and so long as there is no unusual withdrawing of accounts the insolvent condition may be covered up. Many uneasy depositors would like to get their money out if they could do so secretly, or without incurring the displeasure of the others. Meanwhile all insist that the bank is perfectly safe and each does all he can to compel the others to stay in. The thing they all most fear is that some one will "start a run on the bank," force it to liquidate, and everyone will lose. So the crowd functions in its way just so long as its members may be cajoled into an appearance of continued confidence in its ideals and values. The spiritual capital of each depends on the confidence of the others. As a consequence they all spend most of their time exhorting one another to be good crowdmen, fearing and hating no one so much as the person who dares raise the question whether the crowd could really meet its obligations.

The classic illustration of the manner in which the crowd is led to discredit the witness to values contrary to its own, is the oration of Mark Antony in Shakespeare's "Julius Cæsar." It is by this means alone that Antony is able to turn the minds of the Roman citizens into the crowd state. It will be remembered that the address of Brutus, just before this, while not at all a bit of crowd-oratory, left a favorable impression. The citizens are convinced that "This Cæsar was a tyrant."

130

When Antony goes up to speak, he thanks them "for Brutus' sake." They say, "'Twere best he speak no harm of Brutus here." He can never make them his crowd unless he can destroy Brutus' influence. This is precisely what he proceeds gradually to do.

At first with great courtesy—"The noble Brutus hath told you Cæsar was ambitious; if it were so it was a grievous fault . . . for Brutus is an honorable man, so are they all, all honorable men." This sentence is repeated four times in the first section; Cæsar was a good faithful friend to Antony, "But . . . and Brutus is an honorable man." Again Cæsar refused the crown, but "Brutus is an honorable man." Cæsar wept when the poor cried, "sure, Brutus is an honorable man, I speak not to disprove what he says" but "men have lost their reason" and "my heart is in the coffin there with Cæsar." The citizens are sorry for the weeping Antony; they listen more intently now. Again—"If I were disposed to stir your hearts and minds to mutiny and rage"—but that would be to wrong Brutus and Cassius, "Who you all know are honorable men"—this time said with more marked irony. Rather than wrong such honorable men, Antony prefers to "wrong the dead, to wrong myself—and you." That sentence sets Brutus squarely in opposition to the speaker and his audience. Cæsar's will is mentioned—if only the commons knew what was in it, but Antony will not read it, "you are not wood, you are not stones, but men." The speaker now resists their demand to hear the will, he ought not have mentioned it. He fears he has, after all, wronged "the honorable men whose daggers have stabbed Cæsar." The citizens have caught the note of irony now; the honorable men are "traitors," "villains," "murderers."

From this point on the speaker's task is easy; they have become a crowd. They think only of revenge, of killing everyone of the conspirators, and burning the house of Brutus. Antony has even to remind them of the existence of the will. The mischief is set afloat the moment Brutus is successfully discredited.

The development of the thought in this oration is typical. Analysis of almost any propagandist speech will reveal some, if not all, the steps by which Brutus is made an object of hatred. *The crowd hates in order that it may believe in itself.*

VI

THE ABSOLUTISM OF THE CROWD-MIND

WHEREVER conscious thinking is determined by unconscious mechanisms, and all thinking is more or less so, it is dogmatic in character. Beliefs which serve an unconscious purpose do not require the support of evidence. They persist because they are demanded. This is a common symptom of various forms of psychoneurosis. Ideas "haunt the mind" of the patient; he cannot rid himself of them. He may know they are foolish, but he is compelled to think them. In severe cases, he may hear voices or experience other hallucinations which are symbolic of the obsessive ideas. Or his psychic life may be so absorbed by his one fixed idea that it degenerates into the ceaseless repetition of a gesture or a phrase expressive of this idea.

In paranoia the fixed ideas are organized into a system. Brill says:

I know a number of paranoiacs who went through a stormy period lasting for years, but who now live contentedly as if in another world. Such transformations of the world are common in paranoia. They do not care for anything, as nothing is real to them. They have withdrawn their sum of libido from the persons of their environment and the outer world. The end of the world is the projection of this internal catastrophe. Their subjective world came to an end since they withdrew their love from it. By a secondary rationalization, the patients then explain whatever obtrudes itself upon them as something intangible and fit it in with their own system. Thus one of my patients who considers himself a sort of Messiah denies the reality of his own parents by saying that they are only shadows made by his enemy, the devil, whom he has not yet wholly subdued. Another paranoiac in the Central Islip State Hospital, who represented himself as a second Christ, spends most of his time sewing out on cloth crude scenes containing many buildings, interspersed with pictures of the doctors. He explained all this very minutely as the *new world system.* . . . Thus the paranoiac builds up again with his delusions a new world in which he can live. . . . (Italics mine.)

However, a withdrawal of libido is not an exclusive occurrence in paranoia, nor is its occurrence anywhere necessarily followed by disastrous consequences. Indeed, in normal life there is a constant withdrawal of libido from persons and objects without resulting in paranoia or other neuroses. It merely causes a special psychic mood. The withdrawal of the libido as such cannot therefore be considered as pathogenic of paranoia. It requires a special character to distinguish the paranoiac withdrawal of libido from other kinds of the same process. This is readily found when we follow the further utilization of the libido thus withdrawn. Normally, we immediately seek a substitute for the suspended attachment, and until one is found the libido floats freely in the psyche and causes tensions which influence our moods. In hysteria the freed sum of libido becomes transformed into bodily innervations of fear. Clinical indications teach us that in paranoia a special use is made of the libido which is withdrawn from its object ... the freed libido in paranoia is thrown back on the ego and serves to magnify it.

Note the fact that there is a necessary relation between the fixed ideal system of the paranoiac and his withdrawal of interest in the outside world. The system gains the function of reality for him in the same measure that, loving not the world nor the things that are in the world, he has rendered our common human world unreal. His love thrown back upon himself causes him to create another world, a world of "pure reason," so to speak, which is more congenial to him than the world of empirical fact. In this system he takes refuge and finds peace at last. Now we see the function, at least so far as paranoia is concerned, of the ideal system. As Brill says, it is a curative process of a mind which has suffered "regression" or turning back of its interest from the affairs of ordinary men and women, to the attachments of an earlier stage in its history. To use a philosophical term, the paranoiac is the Simon-pure "solipsist." And as *a priori* thinking tends, as Schiller has shown, ever to solipsism, we see here the grain of truth in G. K. Chesterton's witty comparison of rationalism and lunacy.

"Regression," or withdrawal of the libido, is present to some degree I believe in all forms of the neurosis. But we are informed that a withdrawal of the libido may, and frequently does, occur also in normal people. Knowledge of the neurosis here, as elsewhere, serves to throw light on certain thought processes of people who are considered normal. Brill says that "normally we seek a substitute for the suspended attachment." New interests and new affections in time take the places of the objects from which the feelings have been torn. In analytical psychology the process by which this is achieved is called a "transference."

Now the crowd is in a sense a "transference phenomenon." In the temporary crowd or mob this transference is too transitory to be very evident, though even here I believe there will generally be found a certain *esprit de corps*. In permanent crowds there is often a marked transference to the other members of the group. This is evident in the joy of the new convert or the newly initiated, also in such terms of affection as "comrade" and "brother." I doubt, however, if this affection, so far as it is genuine among individuals of a certain crowd, is very different from the good will and affection which may spring up anywhere among individuals who are more or less closely associated, or that it ever really extends beyond the small circle of personal friends that everyone normally gains through his daily relations with others.

But to the crowd-mind this transference is supposed to extend to all the members of the group; they are comrades and brothers not because we like them and know them intimately, but because they are fellow members. In other words, this transference, so far as it is a crowd phenomenon as such, is not to other individuals, but to the idea of the crowd itself. It is not enough for the good citizen to love his neighbors in so far as he finds them lovable; he must love his country. To the churchman the Church herself is an object of faith and adoration. One does not become a humanitarian by being a good fellow; he must love "humanity"—which is to say, the bare abstract idea of everybody. I remember once asking a missionary who was on his way to China what it was that impelled him to go so far in order to minister to suffering humanity. He answered, "It is love." I asked again, "Do you really mean to say that you care so much as that for Chinese, not one of whom you have ever seen?" He answered, "Well, I—you see, I love them through Jesus Christ." So in a sense it is with the crowd-man always; he loves *through the crowd*.

The crowd idealized as something sacred,

as end in itself, as something which it is an honor to belong to, is to some extent a disguised object of our self-love. But the idea of the crowd disguises more than self-love. Like most of the symbols through which the unconscious functions, it can serve more than one purpose at a time. The idea of the crowd also serves to disguise the parental image, and our own imaginary identification or reunion with it. The nation is to the crowd-man the "Fatherland," the "mother country," "Uncle Sam"—a figure which serves to do more than personalize for cartoonists the initials U. S. Uncle Sam is also the father-image thinly disguised. The Church is "the Mother," again the "Bride." Such religious symbols as "the Heavenly Father" and the "Holy Mother" also have the value of standing for the parent image. For a detailed discussion of these symbols, the reader is referred to Jung's *Psychology of the Unconscious.*

In another connection I have referred to the fact that the crowd stands to the member *in loco parentis.* Here I wish to point out the fact that such a return to the parent image is commonly found in the psychoneurosis and is what is meant by "regression." I have also dwelt at some length on the fact that it is by securing a modification in the immediate social environment, ideally or actually, that

crowds. People will wherever possible change the discussion of a mooted question into an antiphonal chorus of howling mobs, each chanting its ritual as ultimate truth, and hurling its shibboleths in the faces of the others. Pursuit of truth with most people consists in repeating their creed. Nearly every movement is immediately made into a cult. Theology supplants religion in the churches. In popular ethics a dead formalism puts an end to moral advance. Straight thinking on political subjects is subordinated to partisan ends. Catch-phrases and magic formulas become substituted for scientific information. Even the Socialists, who feel that they are the intellectually elect—and I cite them here as an example in no unfair spirit, but just because so many of them are really well-informed and "advanced" in their thinking—have been unable to save themselves from a doctrinaire economic orthodoxy of spirit which is often more dogmatic and intolerant than that of the "religious folks" to whose alleged "narrow-mindedness" every Socialist, even while repeating his daily chapter from the Marxian Koran, feels himself superior.

The crowd-mind is everywhere idealistic, and absolutist. Its truths are "given," made-in-advance. Though unconsciously its systems of logic are created to enhance the self-feeling, they appear to consciousness as highly impersonal and abstract. As in the intellectualist philosophies, forms of thought are regarded as themselves objects of thought. Systems of general ideas are imposed upon the minds of men apparently from without. Universal acceptance is demanded. Thought becomes stereotyped. What ought to be is confused with what is, the ideal becomes more real than fact.

In the essays on "Pragmatism" William James showed that the rationalist system, even that of the great philosopher, is in large measure determined by the thinker's peculiar "temperament." Elsewhere he speaks of the "Sentiment of Rationality." For a discussion of the various types of philosophical rationalism, the reader is referred to the criticisms by William James, F. C. S. Schiller, Dewey, and other Pragmatists. It is sufficient for our purpose to note the fact that the rationalist type of mind everywhere shows a tendency to assert the unreality of the world of everyday experience, and to seek comfort and security in the contemplation of a logically ordered system or world of "pure reason." Ideals, not concrete things, are the true realities. The world with which we are always wrestling is but a distorted manifestation, a jumbled, stereotyped copy of what James ironically referred to as "the de luxe

edition which exists in the Absolute." The
parable of the cave which Plato gives in the
Republic represents ordinary knowledge as a
delusion, and the empirically known world as
but dancing shadows on the wall of our
subterranean prison.

R. W. Livingstone, who sees in Platonism,
from the very beginning, a certain world-
weariness and turning away of the Greek
spirit from the healthy realism which had
formerly characterized it, says:

For if Greece showed men how to trust their own
nature and lead a simply human life, how to look
straight in the face of the world and read the beauty
that met them on the surface, certain Greek writers
preached a different lesson from this. In opposition
to directness they taught us to look past the "unimag-
inary and actual" qualities of things to secondary
meanings and inner symbolism. In opposition to
liberty and humanism they taught us to mistrust our
nature, to see in it weakness, helplessness, and incur-
able taint, to pass beyond humanity to communion
with God, to live less for this world than for one to
come. . . . Perhaps to some people it may seem surprising
that this writer is Plato.

According to this view reality may be found
only by means of "pure knowledge," and, to
give a familiar quotation from the Phædo:

If we would have pure knowledge of anything we
must be quit of the body; the soul in herself must

behold things in themselves; and then we shall attain the wisdom which we desire and of which we say that we are lovers; not while we live, but after death; for if, while in company with the body, the soul cannot have pure knowledge, one of two things follows—either knowledge is not to be obtained at all, or if at all after death.

Intellectualism may not always be so clearly other-worldly as Plato shows himself to be in this passage. But it commonly argues that behind the visible world of "illusory sense experience" lies the true ground and cause—an unseen order in which the contradictions of experience are either unknown or harmonized, an external and unchangeable "Substance," a self-contained Absolute to which our ephemeral personalities with their imperfections and problems are unknown. A "thing in itself," or principle of Being which transcends our experience.

This type of thinking, whether it be known as Idealism, Rationalism, Intellectualism, or Absolutism, finds little sympathy from those who approach the study of philosophy from the standpoint of psychology. The following passages taken from *Studies in Humanism* by Schiller, show that even without the technique of the analytical method, it was not hard to detect some of the motives which prompted the construction of systems of this sort. The partisanism of one of these motives is rather suggestive for our study of the mind of the crowd. Says our author:

Logical defects rarely kill beliefs to which men, for psychological reasons, remain attached. . . . This may suggest to us that we may have perhaps unwittingly misunderstood Absolutism, and done it a grave injustice. . . . What if its real appeal was not logical but psychological? . . .

The history of English Absolutism distinctly bears out these anticipations. It was originally a deliberate importation from Germany, with a purpose. And this purpose was a religious one—that of counteracting the antireligious developments of Science. The indigenous philosophy, the old British empiricism, was useless for this purpose. For though a form of intellectualism, its sensationalism was in no wise hostile to Science. On the contrary, it showed every desire to ally itself with, and to promote, the great scientific movement of the nineteenth century, which penetrated into and almost overwhelmed Oxford between 1859 and 1870.

But this movement excited natural and not unwarranted alarm in that great center of theology. For Science, flushed with its hard-won liberty, ignorant of philosophy, and as yet unconscious of its proper limitations, was decidedly aggressive and overconfident. It seemed naturalistic, nay, materialistic, by the law of its being. The logic of Mill, the philosophy of Evolution, the faith in democracy, in freedom, in progress (on material lines), threatened to carry all before them.

What was to be done? Nothing directly; for on its own ground Science seemed invulnerable, and had the knack of crushing the subtlest dialectics by the knock-down force of sheer scientific fact. But might it not be possible to change the venue, to shift the battle-ground to a region *ubi instabilis terra unda* (where the land afforded no firm footing), where the frozen sea could not be navigated, where the very air was thick with mists so that phantoms might well pass for realities—the realm, in short, of metaphysics? . . .

So it was rarely necessary to do more than recite the august table of *a priori* categories in order to make the most audacious scientist feel that he had got out of his depth; while at the merest mention of the Hegelian dialectic all the "advanced thinkers" of the time would flee affrighted.

Schiller's sense of humor doubtless leads him to exaggerate somewhat the deliberateness of this importation of German metaphysics. That these borrowed transcendental and dialectical systems served their purpose in the warfare of traditional theologies against Science is but half the truth. The other half is that these logical formulas provided certain intelligent believers with a defense, or safe refuge, in their own inner conflicts.

That this is the case, Schiller evidently has little doubt. After discussing Absolutism itself as a sort of religion, and showing that its "catch-words" taken at their face value are not only emotionally barren, but also logically meaningless because "inapplicable to our actual experience," he then proceeds to an examination of the unconscious motives which determine this sort of thinking. His description of these motives, so far as it goes, is an excellent little bit of analytical psychology. He says:

How then can Absolutism possibly be a religion? It must appeal to psychological motives of a different sort, rare enough to account for its total divergence from the ordinary religious feelings and compelling enough to account for the fanaticism with which it is held and the persistence with which the same old round of negations has been reiterated through the ages. Of such psychological motives we shall indicate the more important and reputable.

(1) It is decidedly flattering to one's spiritual pride to feel oneself a "part" or "manifestation" or "vehicle" or "reproduction" of the Absolute Mind, and to some this feeling affords so much strength and comfort and such exquisite delight that they refrain from inquiring what these phrases mean. . . . It is, moreover, the strength of this feeling which explains the blindness of Absolutists toward the logical defects of their own theory. . . .

(2) There is a strange delight in wide generalization merely as such, which, when pursued without reference to the ends which it subserves, and without regard to its actual functioning, often results in a sort of logical vertigo. This probably has much to do with the peculiar "craving for unity" which is held to be the distinctive affliction of philosophers. At any rate, the thought of an all-embracing One or Whole seems to be regarded as valuable and elevating quite apart from any definite function it performs in knowing, or light it throws on any actual problem.

(3) The thought of an Absolute Unity is cherished as a guarantee of cosmic stability. In face of the restless vicissitudes of phenomena it seems to secure us against falling out of the Universe. It assures us *a*

priori—and that is its supreme value—that the cosmic order cannot fall to pieces and leave us dazed and confounded among the debris. . . . We want to have an absolute assurance *a priori* concerning the future, and the thought of the absolute seems designed to give it. It is probably this last notion that, consciously or unconsciously, weighs most in the psychology of the Absolutists' creed.

In this connection the reader will recall the passage quoted from Adler's *The Neurotic Constitution*, in which it was shown that the fictitious "guiding-lines" or rational systems of both the neurotic and normal are motivated by this craving for security. But it makes all the difference in the world whether the system of ideas is used, as in science and common sense, to solve real problems in an objective world, or is created to be an artificial and imaginary defense of the ego against a subjective feeling of insecurity; whether, in a word, the craving for security moves one to do something calculated to render the forces with which he must deal concretely more congenial and hospitable to his will, or makes him content to withdraw and file a demur to the challenge of the environment in the form of theoretical denial of the reality of the situation.

There is no denying the fact that Absolute Idealism, if not taken too seriously, may have the function for some people of steadying their nerves in the battle of life. And though, as I believe, logically untenable, it not infrequently serves as a rationalization of faith-values which work out beneficially, and, quite apart from their metaphysical trappings, may be even indispensable. Yet when carried to its logical conclusions such thinking inevitably distorts the meaning of personal living, robs our world and our acts of their feeling of reality, serves as an instrument for "regression" or withdrawal of interest from the real tasks and objects of living men and women, and in fact functions for much the same purpose, if not precisely in the same way, as do the ideal systems of the psychopath.

In justice to idealism it should be added that this is by no means the only species of Rationalism which may lead to such psychic results. There are various paths by which the craving for artificial security may lead to such attempts to reduce the whole of possible experience to logical unity that the realities of time and change and of individual experience are denied. How many deterministic theories, with all their scientific jargon, are really motivated by an inability to accept a world with an element of chance in it. There is a sense in which all science by subsuming like individuals in a common class, and thus ignoring their individuality, in so far as they are alike in certain respects, gains added power over all of them. There is a sense, too, in which science, by discovering that whenever a given combination of elements occurs, a definitely foreseen result will follow, is justified in ignoring time and treating certain futures as if they were already tucked up the sleeves of the present. It should be remembered that this sort of determinism is purely methodological, and is, like all thinking, done for a purpose—that of effecting desirable ends in a world made up of concrete situations.

When this purpose becomes supplanted by a passion to discount all future change in general—when one imagines that he has a formula which enables him to write the equation of the curve of the universe, science has degenerated into scientificism, or head-in-the-sand philosophy. The magic formula has precisely the same psychic value as the "absolute." I know a number of economic determinists, for instance, who just cannot get out of their heads the notion that social evolution is a process absolutely underwritten, guaranteed, and predictable, without the least possible doubt. In such a philosophy of history as this the individual is of course a mere "product of his environment," and his role as a creator of value is nil. On this "materialistic" theory, the individual is as truly a mere manifestation of impersonal evolutionary forces as he is, according to orthodox Platonism, a mere manifestation of the abstract idea of his species. Notwithstanding the professed impersonalism of this view, its value for consolation in minimizing the causes of the spiritual difference in men —that is, its function for enhancing the self-feeling of some people, is obvious. That such an idea should become a crowd-idea is not to be wondered at. And this leads me to my point. *It is no mere accident that the crowd takes to rationalistic philosophies like a duck to water.*

The crowd-man, however unsophisticated he may be, is a Platonist at heart. He may never have heard the word epistemology, but his theory of knowledge is essentially the same as Plato's. Religious crowds are, to one familiar with the Dialogues, astonishingly Platonic. There is the same habit of giving ontological rather than functional value to general ideas, the same other-worldliness, the same moral dilemmas, the same contempt for the material, for the human body, for selfhood; the same assertion of finality, and the conformist spirit.

Reformist crowds differ only superficially from religious crowds. Patriotic crowds make use of a different terminology, but their mental habits are the same. It has become a cult among crowds with tendencies toward social revolution to paint their faces with the colors of a borrowed nineteenth-century materialism.

151

But all this is mere swagger and "frightfulness," an attempt to make themselves look terrible and frighten the bourgeois. I am sure that no one who has seen all this radical rigmarole, as I have had occasion to see it, can be deceived by it. These dreadful materialist doctrines of the radical crowd are wooden guns, no thicker than the soap-box. As a matter of fact, the radical crowds are extremely idealistic. With all their talk of proletarian opposition to intellectualism, Socialists never become a crowd without becoming as intellectualist as Fichte or Hegel. There is a sense in which Marx himself never succeeded in escaping Hegel's dilemmas, he only followed the fashion in those days of turning them upside down.

With radical crowds as with conservative, there is the same substitution of a closed system of ideas for the shifting phenomena of our empirical world; the same worship of abstract forms of thought, the same uncompromising spirit and insistence upon general uniformity of opinions; the same orthodoxy. All orthodoxy is nothing other than the will of the crowd to keep itself together. With all kinds of crowds, also, there is the same diverting of attention from the personal and the concrete to the impersonal and the general; the same flight from reality to the transcendental for escape, for consolation, for defense, for vindication; the same fiction that existence is at bottom a sort of logical proposition, a magic formula or principle of Being to be correctly copied and learned by rote; the same attempt to create the world or find reality by thinking rather than by acting.

The intellectualist bias of the average man is doubtless due in great part to the fact that theology, and therefore the religious education of the young, both Christian and Jewish, has throughout the history of these religions been saturated with Platonism. But then, the universal sway of this philosopher may be explained by the fact that there is something in his abstractionism which is congenial to the creed-making propensities of the crowd-mind. The great *a priori* thinkers, Plato, St. Augustine, Thomas Aquinas, Anselm, Rousseau, Kant, Hegel, Green, etc., have often been called solitary men, but it is significant that their doctrines survive in popularized form in the creeds and shibboleths of permanent crowds of all descriptions. While humanists, nominalists, empiricists, realists, pragmatists, men like Protagoras, Epicurus, Abelard, Bacon, Locke, Hume, Schopenhauer, Nietzsche, Bergson, James, have always had a hard time of it. They are considered destructive, for the reason that the tendency of their teaching is to disintegrate the crowd-mind and call one back to himself. Their names are seldom mentioned in popular assemblies except to discredit them. Yet it is on the whole these latter thinkers who orient us in our real world, make us courageously face the facts with which we have to deal, stimulate our wills, force us to use our ideas for what they are—instruments for better living,—inspire us to finer and more correct valuations of things, and point out the way to freedom for those who dare walk in it.

All this, however, is the very thing that the crowd-mind is running headlong away from. As a crowd we do not wish to think empirically. Why should we seek piecemeal goods by tedious and dangerous effort, when we have only to do a little trick of attention, and behold The Good, abstract, perfect, universal, waiting just around the corner in the realm of pure reason, ready to swallow up and demolish all evil? Are we not even now in possession of Love, Justice, Beauty, and Truth by the sheer magic of thinking of them in the abstract, calling them "principles" and writing the words with the initial letters in capitals? The very mental processes by which a group of people becomes a crowd change such abstract nouns from mere class names into copies of supermundane realities.

In wholesome thinking principles are of course necessary. They are what I might call "leading ideas." Their function is to lead to more satisfactory thinking—that is, to other ideas which are desired. Or they are useful in leading us to actions the results of which are intended and wished for. They may also be principles of valuation guiding us in the choice of ends. If there were no substantial agreement among us concerning certain principles we could not relate our conduct to one another at all; social life would be impossible. But necessary as such leading ideas are, they are means rather than ends. Circumstances may demand that we alter them or make exceptions to their application.

To the crowd-mind a principle appears as an end in itself. It must be vindicated at all costs. To offend against it in one point is to be guilty of breaking the whole law. Crowds are always uncompromising about their principles. They must apply to all alike. Crowds are no respecters of persons.

As crowd-men we never appear without some set of principles or some cause over our heads. Crowds crawl under their principles like worms under stones. They cover up the wrigglings of the unconscious, and protect it from attack. Every crowd uses its principles as universal demands. In this way it gets unction upon other crowds, puts them in the wrong, makes them give assent to the crowd's real purpose by challenging them to deny the righteousness of the professed justifications of that purpose. It is said that the Sioux Indians, some years ago, used to put their women and children in front of their firing line. The braves could then crouch behind these innocent ones and shoot at white men, knowing that it would be a violation of the principles of humanity for the white soldiers to shoot back and risk killing women and children. Crowds frequently make just such use of their principles. About each crowd, like the circle of fire which the gods placed about the sleeping Brunhilde, there is a flaming hedge of logical abstractions, sanctions, taboos, which none but the intellectually courageous few dare cross. In this way the slumbering critical faculties of the crowd-mind are protected against the intrusion of realities from outside the cult. The intellectual curiosity of the members of the group is kept within proper bounds. Hostile persons or groups dare not resist us, for in so doing they make themselves enemies of Truth, of Morality, of Liberty, etc. Both political parties, by a common impulse, "drape themselves in the Flag." It is an interesting fact that the most antagonistic crowds profess much the same set of principles. The "secondary rationalization" of crowds, both Northern and Southern, at the time of the Civil War, made use of our traditional principles of American Liberty, and Christian

Morality. We have seen both pacifist and militarist crowds setting forth their manifestoes in terms of New Testament teaching. Each religious sect exists only to teach "the one system of doctrine logically deduced from Scripture."

As an illustration of this sort of reasoning, I give here a few passages from a propagandist publication in which the crowd-will to dominate takes the typical American method of striving to force its cult ideas upon the community as a whole by means of restrictive moralist legislation—in this case attempt is made to prohibit the exhibition of motion pictures on Sunday. That the demand for such legislation is for the most part a pure class-crowd phenomenon, designed to enhance the self-feeling and economic interests of the "reformers," by keeping the poor from having a good time, is I think, rather obvious. The reasoning here is interesting, as the real motive is so thinly disguised by pietistic platitudes that the two follow each other in alternate succession:

(1) Sunday Movies are not needed. The people have six days and six nights each week on which to attend the movies. Is not that plenty of time for all?

(2) Sunday Movie Theaters commercialize the Christian Sabbath. While "the Sabbath was made for man," *yet it is God's day.* We have no right to sell it for business purposes. It is a day for rest and worship,

THE BEHAVIOR OF CROWDS

not a day for greed and gain. Sunday would, of course, be the best day in the week financially for the movies. It would also be the best day in the week for the open saloons and horse-racing, but that is no reason why these should be allowed on Sunday. *The Sabbath must not be commercialized.*

(3) *Sunday Movie Theaters destroy the rest and quiet of many people, especially those who live in the residential district* of cities and in the neighborhood where such motion-picture theaters are located. Great crowds pour along the streets near such theaters, often breaking the Sunday quiet of that part of the city by loud and boisterous talk.

Thousands of people every year are moving away from the downtown noisy districts of the cities out into the quiet residential districts in order to have quiet Sundays. But when a motion-picture theater comes and locates next to their homes, or in their block, as has been done in many cases, and great noisy, boisterous crowds surge back and forth before their homes all Sunday afternoon and evening, going to the movies, they are being robbed of *that for which they paid their money when they bought a home in that quiet part of the city.* . . .

(4) . . . Anything that injures the Christian Sabbath injures the Christian churches, and certainly Sunday motion-picture theaters, wherever allowed, do injure the Christian Sabbath. . . .

Dr. Wilbur F. Crafts of Washington, D. C., probably the greatest authority on the Sabbath question in this country, says, "The Sabbath-keeping nations are the strongest physically, mentally, morally, *financially*, and politically." Joseph Cook said, "It is no accident that the nations that keep the Sabbath most carefully are those where there is the most political freedom." *Sabbath-breaking nations gradually lose their political freedom.*

(5) Sunday Movie Theaters injure the Christian Sabbath and thus injure the morals of the people. *Anything that injures the morals of the people, injures the nation itself.* From a *patriotic* standpoint, we ought to stand for strict observance of the Christian Sabbath, as past experience has shown and the testimony of many witnesses proves that a disregard of the Christian Sabbath produces crime and immorality and tends to destroy the free institutions which have helped to make our nation great. . . .

Fundamentally, all such vicious laws are *unconstitutional.*

Sunday Movie Theaters disregard the rights of labor . . . . Canon William Sheafe Chase has aptly said, "No man has the Christ spirit who wants a better time on Sunday than he is willing to give everyone else." . . .

Col. Fairbanks, the famous scale manufacturer, said: "I can tell by watching the men at work Monday which spent Sunday in sport and which at home, church, or Sabbath-school. The latter *do more and better work.*"

Superintendents of large factories in Milwaukee and elsewhere have said, "When our men go on a Sunday excursion, some cannot work Monday, and many who work cannot earn their wages, while *those who had no sport Sunday do their best day's work Monday.*" (Italics mine.)

We need not be surprised to find that the closed ideational system which in the first instance is a refuge from the real, becomes in turn a device for imposing one's will upon his fellows. The believer's ego is served in both instances. It is interesting to note also that this self-feeling appears in crowd-thinking as its very opposite. *The greatest enemy of per-*

sonality is the crowd. The crowd does not want valuable men; it wants only useful men. Everyone must justify his existence by appealing to the not-self. One may do nothing for his own sake. He may not even strive for spiritual excellence for such a reason. He must live for "principle," for "the great cause," for impersonal abstractions—which is to say, he must live for his crowd, and so make it easier for the other members to do the same with a good face.

The complex of ideas in which the crowd-mind as we have seen takes refuge, being necessarily made up of abstract generalizations, serves the crowd-will to social dominance through the very claim to universality which such ideas exert. Grant that an idea is an absolute truth, and it follows, of course, that it must be true on all occasions and for everyone. The crowd is justified, therefore, in sacrificing people to its ideal—itself. The idea is no longer an instrument of living; it is an imperative. It is not yours to use the idea; the idea is there to use you. You have ceased to be an end. Anything about you that does not partake of the reality of this idea has no right to be, any experience of yours which happens to be incommensurable with this idea loses its right to be; for experience as such has now only a "phenomenal existence." The crowd, by identifying its will to

160

power with this idea, becomes *itself absolute*. Your personal self, as an end, is quite as unwelcome to the Absolute as to the crowd. There must be no private property in thought or motive. By making everybody's business my business, I have made my business everybody's business. There may be only one standard—that of our crowd, which, because of its very universal and impersonal character is really nobody's.

The absolutism of the crowd-mind with its consequent hostility to conscious personality finds a perfect rationalization in the ethical philosophy of Kant. The absolutism of the idea of Duty is less skillfully elaborated in its popular crowd-manifestations, but in its essentials it is always present, as propaganda everywhere when carefully annalyzed will show. We must not be deceived by Kant's assertion that the individual is an end. This individual is not you or I, or anyone; it is a mere logical abstraction. By declaring that everyone is equally an end, Kant ignores all personal differences, and therefore the fact of individuality as such. We are each an end in respect to those qualities only in which we are identical—namely, in that we are "rational beings." But this rational being is not a personal intelligence; it is a fiction, a bundle of mental faculties assumed *a priori* to exist, and then treated as if it were universally and equally applicable to all actually existing intelligences.

In arguing that "I am never to act otherwise than so that I could also will that my maxim should become a universal law," Kant may be easily understood as justifying any crowd in seeking to make its peculiar maxims universal laws. Who but a Rationalist or a crowd-man presumes to have found the "universal law," who else would have the effrontery to try to legislate for every conscience in existence? But this presumption has its price. In thus universalizing my moral will, I wholly depersonalize it. He says:

It is of extreme importance to remember that we must not allow ourselves to think of deducing the reality of this principle from the particular attributes of human nature. For duty is to be a practical unconditional necessity of action; it must therefore hold for all rational beings (to whom an imperative can apply at all), and for this reason only be also a law for all human wills. On the contrary, whatever it deduces from the particular natural characteristics of humanity, from certain feelings and propensions, nay, even if possible from any particular tendency proper to human reason, and which need not necessarily hold for the will of every rational being, this may indeed supply us with a maxim but not with a law; with a subjective principle on which we may have a propension or inclination to act, but not with an objective principle on which we should be *enjoined* to act, *even though all our propensions, inclinations, and natural dispositions were opposed* to it. In fact, the *sublimity and intrinsic dig-*

nity of the command in duty *are so much the more evident the less subjective impulses favor it, and the more they oppose it* [italics here are mine], without being able in the slightest degree to weaken the obligation of the law or to diminish its validity.

. . . An action done from duty derives its moral worth *not from the purpose* which is to be attained by it, but from the maxim by which it is determined. It (this moral worth) cannot lie anywhere but in the *principle of The Will*, without regard to the ends which can be attained by such action.

This loss of the conscious self in the universal, this turning away from the empirically known, this demand that an *a priori* principle be followed to its deadly practical conclusion *regardless of the ends* to which it leads, is of utmost importance for our study. It is precisely what the paranoiac does after his own fashion. In crowd-thinking it is often made the instrument of wholesale destruction and human slaughter. The mob is ever motivated by this logic of negation, and of automatic behavior. It is thus that compulsive thinking sways vast hordes of men and women, impelling them, in the very name of truth or righteousness, to actions of the most atrocious character. It is this which robs most popular movements of their intelligent purposiveness, unleashes the fanatic and the bigot, and leads men to die and to kill for a phrase. This way of thinking points straight to Salem, Massachusetts, to the torture-chamber, the pile of fagots and the mill pond at Rosmersholm.

The habit of thinking as a crowd is so widespread that it is impossible to trace the influence of its rationalistic negations in the daily mental habits of most of us. We play out our lives as if we were but acting a part which some one had assigned to us. The fact that we are ourselves realities, as inevitable as falling rain, and with the same right to be as the rocks and hills, positively startles us. We feel that we must plead extenuation, apologize for our existence, as if the end and aim of living were to serve or vindicate a Good which, being sufficient in itself and independent of us, can never be realized as actually good for anybody. We behave as if we were unprofitable servants, cringing before wrathful ideas which, though our own creations, we permit to lord it over us. Our virtues we regard not as expressions of ourselves or as habitual ways of reaching desirable goods, but as if they were demanded of us unwillingly by something not self. We should remind ourselves that these big words we idolize have no eyes to see us and no hearts to care what we do, that they are but symbols of ideas which we might find very useful if we dared to become masters of them. The most common use we make of such ideas is to beat one another and ourselves into line with them, or enforce upon ourselves and others the collection of a debt which was contracted only by our unconscious desire to cheat at cards in the game of civilization.

A conscious recognition of this desire and its more deliberate and voluntary resistance in ourselves rather than in our neighbors, a candid facing of the fact of what we really are and really want, and a mutual readjustment of our relations on this recognized basis would doubtless deliver us from the compulsion of crowd-thinking in somewhat the same way that psychoanalysis is said to cure the neurotic by revealing to him his unconscious wish.

That some such cure is an imperative social need is evident. To-day the mob lurks just under the skin of most of us, both ignorant and educated. The ever-increasing frequency of outbreaks of mob violence has its source in the crowd-thinking which is everywhere encouraged. The mob which may at any time engulf us is, after all, but the logical conclusion and sudden ripening of thought processes which are commonly regarded as highly respectable, idealistic, and moral.

VII

THE PSYCHOLOGY OF REVOLUTIONARY CROWDS

THE crowd-mind is seen at its best and at its worst in revolution. To many minds, revolution is so essentially a crowd phenomenon that the terms revolution and crowd-rule are almost synonymous. "Hurrah, the mob rules Russia," cried certain radicals in the spring of 1917—"Let the people rule everywhere." Others, more conservative, saw in every extravagant deed and atrocity alleged to have happened in Russia only the thing logically to be expected where the mob rules. The idea of revolution is itself so commonly a crowd-idea that the thinking—if thinking it may be called—of most people on this subject depends principally upon which crowd we happen to belong to, the crowd which sustains the ego-feeling of its members by the hope of revolution, or the crowd which, for similar reason, brands everything which opposes its interests, real or imaginary, as "anarchy" and "Bolshevism."

If the word "revolution" be taken to

mean fundamental change in men's habits of thought, and life, and the forms of their relations to one another, then it may be said that great "revolutions may be and have been achieved with a relatively small degree of crowd-thinking and mob violence." Much of the normal development of civilization, for instance, the great scientific advance of the nineteenth century, the spread of culture, the creation of artistic values, the rise in the standard of living, is change of this sort. Such change is, however, gradual. It is brought about by countless concrete adaptations, by thinking always toward realizable ends. New and often unforeseeable results are thus reached; but they are reached, as in all organic growth and in all sound thinking, by a series of successful adjustments within the real. True progress is doubtless made up of changes of this sort. But for the course of progress to run on uninterrupted and un-defeated we should have to be, both in our individual and social behavior, the reasonable beings which certain nineteenth-century utilitarians mistook us for.

It is the fool thing, the insincere thing, that more commonly happens in matters social and political. The adjustment reached is not often a solution of a social problem worked out deliberately on the "greatest-happiness" principle. It is commonly a *status quo*, or balance of power among contending crowds, each inspired by the fiction of its own importance, by self-idealization, and desire to rule. It is an unstable equilibrium usually held in place for the time by a dominant crowd. This dominant crowd may itself be composed of quarreling factions, but these parties, so long as they share enough of the supremacy to keep up their self-feeling, so long, in fact, as their members may even be able to make themselves believe that they, too, are in the upper set, or so long as they continue to hope for success in the social game as now played, unite in repeating the catchwords which justify their crowd in its supremacy. The dominant group identifies its own interests with the general welfare. And in the sense that some sort of order, or any at all, is to be preferred to social chaos, there is an element of truth in this identification.

The fact remains, however, that the dominant crowd possesses always much of the crowd-spirit which originally secured for it its enviable position. Its ideas, like those of all crowds, are devices for sustaining the self-feeling of its members, for protecting itself, for keeping the group together, for justification. They are only secondarily, if at all, instruments for dealing with new and perplexing social situations. It cannot be denied that a certain set of opinions, prejudices, mannerisms, ceremonies "go with" the social position which corresponds to them. They are the ready-made habits of the "set" or class. They are badges by which the "gentleman" is distinguished, the evening clothes of the psyche, as it were. Many of these crowd-forms represent true values of living, some of them are useful in our dealings with reality; if this were not so, if such spiritual tattooings or ceremonial forms were wholly harmful, the crowd which performed them would be at such a disadvantage that it could not hold its own. But that considerations of utility—other than the function which such ceremonialism is known to have for the unconscious always—do not directly govern these forms of thought and behavior is seen in the fact that so many of them, as Sumner says of "folkways," are either harmful or useless in dealing with matters of fact.

The dominant crowd, therefore, in just so far as it must remain a crowd in order to secure its own position of supremacy, must strive to force all social realities into the forms of its own conflicts and dilemmas. Inevitably the self-feeling of a great many people, who are forced by the dominant crowd to conform and labor with no compensation, is hurt. They cannot but contrast their own lot with that of their more fortunate neighbors. Of all things, people probably resist most the feeling of inferiority. Any suggestion that the difference in social position is due to a similar difference in personal worth or in ability is hotly resented. The resentment is in no wise abated by the fact that in some cases this suggestion may be true. Compensations are at once created by the unconscious. In mediæval times "all men were brothers and were equal before the altars of the Church and in heaven." Thus distinctions of merit, other than those which prevailed in the social order, were set up in the interest of the common man.

As the influence of the Renaissance directed general attention from the realm of the spiritual to practical affairs of earth, these compensations changed from thoughts of the future world to dreams of the future of this world. The injured self-feeling dwells upon the economic or political inequalities which flow from the dominance of the ruling crowd. The injustices and acts of exploitation, which are certainly neither new nor rare occurrences in human relations, are seized upon as if it were these things, not the assumption to superiority, which were the issue at stake.

At the time of the French Revolution the Third Estate, or Bourgeois, which showed itself quite as capable of exploiting the poor as ever were the older aristocrats, saw itself only as part of the wronged and exploited "people." The sufferings of the poor, which

170

it was frequently even then profiting in quite as heartily, to say the least, as the titled nobility, were represented as the grievance of all mankind against the hated nobility. That the ideas of "liberty, equality, and fraternity" which these good tradesmen preached may easily become the sort of compensatory ideas we have been discussing is shown by the fact of the genuine astonishment and indignation of the burghers when later their employees made use of this same phrase in the struggles between labor and capital. Sans-culottism had quite as many psychological motives as economic behind it.

How pompous, hateful, and snobbish were those titled folk with their powdered wigs, carriages, fine clothes, and their exclusive social gatherings to which honest citizens, often quite as wealthy as themselves, were not invited. If the "people"—that is, the burghers themselves—only had a chance they would be just as fine ladies and gentlemen as those who merely inherited their superiority. Down with the aristocrats! All men were equal and always had been. There must be fraternity and the *carier ouvert les talents*, in other words, brotherhood and free competition.

I am sure, from all I have ever seen or read of social revolt and unrest, that this injured self-feeling, or defense against the sense of personal inferiority, while not the only motive, is the most powerful one at work. It crops out everywhere, in the layman's hatred of the clergy during the Reformation, in that curious complex of ideas whereby the uneducated often look upon a college diploma as something little short of magical, and defend their ego against this ridiculously exaggerated mark of distinction and accompanying feeling of self-reproach by a slur at "high-brows." Few people realize how general this feeling is; the trick of making fun of the educated is one of the commonest forms of crowd-humor in America, both in vaudeville and in popular oratory. I have previously pointed out the fact that the religious revival in our day is to a great extent characterized by a popular resistance to scholars. No one can read Mr. Sunday's sermons and deny this fact. The City of New York gave the largest majority in its history to the candidate for the office of mayor who made opposition to "experts" the main issue in his campaign. Scores of times I have heard popular speakers resort to this trick to gain favor with their audiences, and I cannot remember ever having known such sentiments to fail to gain applause—I am not speaking now of strictly academic groups, but of general gatherings.

The point of interest here is that these same people have a most extravagant notion of the value of the academic training which they encourage the crowd speaker in ridiculing. I have made it a practice of talking with a great many people personally and drawing them out on this point, and I have found that this is almost uniformly the case. F. B., a cigar maker by trade, says, "Oh, if I had only had sense enough to go on to school when I had the opportunity!" E. L., a mechanic, says, "I might have been somebody, if I had been given any chance to get an education." R., a sort of jack-of-all-trades, says, "If I only had N.'s education, I'd be a millionaire." B., a farmer with limited intellectual interests, says, "I tell you, my boys are not going to be like me; they have got to go to college." G., a waiter, says, "I don't know much," and then proceeds to impress me with the latest bit of academic information which he has picked up. C., a printer, who has been moderately successful, says: "I'd give ten thousand dollars right this minute if I knew Greek; now there is —— and there is ——, neighbors of mine, they're highly educated. When I'm with them I'm ashamed and feel like a dub."

When, on such occasions, I repeatedly say that the average academic student really learns hardly anything at all of the classic languages, and cite the small fruits of my own years of tedious study as an example, the effect produced is invariably comforting—

until I add that one need not attend a university seven years or even four to become educated, but that nearly everyone with ability to learn and with genuine intellectual interests may achieve a remarkable degree of learning. The answer of the perplexed person is then often an extenuation. "Well, you see, a busy person or a working man is so tired after the day's work that he has no energy left for study," or it is, "Wait till the working class have more leisure, then they, too, can be cultivated." Passing over this extenuation, which ignores the fact that some of the best informed and clearest thinking people one meets are working people, while the average university graduate leads anything but an intellectual life, it can hardly be denied, I think, that our crowd cult of anti-"highbrowism" is really a defense mechanism against an inner feeling of inferiority. Now the interesting thing about this feeling of inferiority is the exaggerated notion of the superiority of the college-trained, which is entertained chiefly by the uneducated themselves. What appears here is in fact nothing other than a cheapening of the idea of superiority. Personal excellence is something which anyone may attain; it is not something congenital, but something to be added on; one "gets an education," possesses something of advantage, merely by a few years of conventional study of books. Anyone might do that, therefore. "I, too, if I only cared to, or had been given opportunity, might now be famous." "The difference between myself and the world's greatest genius is not a spiritual chasm which I could not myself, at least hypothetically, cross." "It is rather an 'acquired character,' a mere fruit of special opportunity—which in a few cases it doubtless may be—but it is something external; at bottom we are all equal."

Many facts may be advanced to corroborate the results of our analysis here. The crowd always resents the Carlyle, William James, Nietzsche, Goethe theory of genius. Genius is not congenital superiority. It is the result of hard work. The genius is not a unique personal fact, he is a "representative man." He says just what his age is thinking. The inarticulate message of his contemporaries simply becomes articulate in some one, and behold a genius. In other words, I suppose, all Vienna, messenger boys and bootblacks especially, were suddenly fascinated by Schiller's "Ode to Joy" and went about whistling improvised musical renderings of the theme of this poem, till the deaf Beethoven heard and wrote these whistlings down in the form of the Ninth Symphony.

According to the crowd, Luther did not create the Reformation, or Petrarch the Renaissance; these movements themselves created their leaders and founders; all that the genius did was to interpret and faithfully obey the People's will. Ergo, to be a genius one need only study hard enough to be able to tell the people what they already think. The superiority of genius is therefore no different from that of any educated person; except in degree of application. Anyone of us might possess this superiority. In other words, the "intellectual snobbishness" which the crowd resents is nothing else than the crowd-man's own fiction of self-importance, projected upon those whose imagined superiority he envies. It is recognized, even exaggerated by the unlearned, because it is precisely the sort of superiority which the ignorant man himself, in his ignorance, imagines that he himself would display if he "only had the chance," and even now possesses unrecognized.

We have made the foregoing detour because I think it serves to illustrate, in a way, the psychic processes behind much revolutionary propaganda and activity. I would not attempt to minimize the extent of the social injustice and economic slavery which a dominant crowd, whether ecclesiastical, feudal, or capitalistic, is guilty of in its dealings with its subjects. But every dominant crowd, certain sections of the "proletariat" as quickly as any other, will resort to such practices, and will alike justify them by moral catchwords the minute its supremacy over other crowds gives it opportunity. Therefore there is a certain amount of tautology in denouncing the "master class" for its monstrous abuses. That the real point at issue between the dominant crowd and the under crowd is the assumed personal superiority of the members of the former, rather than the economic "exploitation" which it practices, is shown by the fact that the French Revolution was led by wealthy bourgeois, and that the leading revolutionary element in the working class to-day consists, not of the "down and out" victims of capitalist exploitation, but of the members of the more highly skilled and better paid trades, also of certain intellectuals who are not "proletarians" at all.

And now we come to our point: the fiction of superiority of the dominant crowd, just as in the case of the assumed personal superiority of the intellectuals, is resented by the under crowd because it is *secretly recognized* by the under crowd. Of course the dominant crowd, like all crowds, is obsessed by its feelings of self-importance, and this feeling is apparently vindicated by its very social position. But the fiction is recognized at its full face value, and therefore resented by the under crowds, because that is precisely the sort of personal supremacy to which they also aspire.

One commonly hears it said to-day, by those who have made the catchwords of democracy their crowd cult, that the issue in modern society is between democracy and capitalism. In a sense this may be true, but only in a superficial sense; the real issue is between the personal self as a social entity and the crowd. Capitalism is, to my mind, the logical first fruit of so-called democracy. Capitalism is simply the social supremacy of the trader-man crowd. For a hundred years and more commercial ability—that of organizing industry and selling goods—has been rewarded out of all proportion to any other kind of ability, because, in the first place, it leads to the kind of success which the ordinary man most readily recognizes and envies— large houses, fine clothes, automobiles, exclusive clubs, etc. A Whittier may be ever so great a poet, and yet sit beside the stove in the general store of his little country village, and no one thinks he is so very wonderful. Some may envy him his fame, but few will envy and therefore be fascinated by that in him which they do not understand. But a multimillionaire in their community is understood; everyone can see and envy his success; he is at once both envied and admired.

Moreover, the commercial ability is the sort which the average man most commonly thinks he possesses in some degree. While, therefore, he grumbles at the unjust inequalities in wealth which exist in modern society, and denounces the successful business man as an exploiter and fears his power, the average man will nevertheless endure all this, much in the same spirit that a student being initiated into a fraternity will take the drubbing, knowing well that his own turn at the fun will come later. It is not until the members of the under crowd begin to suspect that their own dreams of "aping the rich" may never come true that they begin to entertain revolutionary ideas. In other words, forced to abandon the hope of joining the present dominating crowd, they begin to dream of supplanting and so dispossessing this crowd by their own crowd.

That the dominant crowd is just as much to blame for this state of affairs as the under crowd, perhaps more so, is shown by the history of every period preceding a revolutionary outbreak. I will dwell at some length on this fact later. My point here is that, first, a revolution, in the sense that the word means a violent uprising against the existing order, is a psychological crowd-phenomenon—and second, that it takes two crowds to make a revolution.

Writers, like Le Bon, have ignored the part which the dominant crowd plays in such events. They have thought of revolution only as the behavior of the under crowd. They have assumed that the crowd and the people were the same. Their writings are hardly more than conservative warnings against the excess and wickedness of the popular mind once it is aroused. Sumner says:

Moral traditions are the guides which no one can afford to neglect. They are in the mores, and they are lost in every great revolution of the mores. Then the men are morally lost.

Le Bon says, writing of the French Revolution:

The people may kill, burn, ravage, commit the most frightful cruelties, glorify its hero to-day and throw him into the gutter to-morrow; it is all one; the politicians will not cease to vaunt its virtues, its high wisdom, and to bow to its every decision.

Now in what does this entity really consist, this mysterious fetich which revolutionists have revered for more than a century?

It may be decomposed into two distinct categories. The first includes the peasants, traders, and workers of all sorts who need tranquillity and order that they may exercise their calling. This people forms the majority, but a majority which never caused a revolution. Living in laborious silence, it is ignored by historians.

The second category, which plays a capital part in all national disturbances, consists of a subversive social residue dominated by a criminal mentality. Degenerates of alcoholism and poverty, thieves, beggars, destitute "casuals," indifferent workers without employment—these constitute the dangerous bulk of the armies of insurrection. . . . To this sinister substratum are due the massacres which stain all revolutions. . . . To elements recruited from the lowest dregs of the populace are added by contagion a host of idle and indifferent persons who are simply drawn into the movement. They shout because there are men shouting, and revolt because there is a revolt, without having the vaguest idea of the cause of the shouting or revolution. The suggestive power of the environment absolutely hypnotized them.

This idea, which is held with some variation by Sumner, Gobineau, Faguet, and Conway, is, I believe, both unhistorical and unpsychological, because it is but a half-truth. This substratum of the population does at the moment of revolution become a dangerous mob. Such people are unadjusted to any social order, and the least deviation from the routine of daily life throws them off their balance. The relaxation of authority at the moment when one group is supplanting another in position of social control, is to these people like the two or three days of interregnum between the pontificates of Julius and Leo, described by Cellini. Those who need some one to govern them, and they are many, find their opportunity in the general disturbance. They suddenly react to the revolutionary propaganda which up to this minute they have not heeded, they are controlled by revolutionary crowd-ideas in a somnambulistic manner, and like automatons carry these ideas precipitately to their deadly conclusion. But this mob is not the really revolutionary crowd and in the end it is always put back in its place by the newly dominant crowd. The really revolutionary crowd consists of the group who are near enough the dominant crowd to be able to envy its "airs" with some show of justification, and are strong enough to dare try issue with it for supreme position. Madame Rolland, it will be remembered, justified her opposition to aristocrats on the principle of equality and fraternity, but she could never forget her resentment at being made, in the home of a member of this aristocracy, to eat with the servants.

What Le Bon and others seem to ignore is that the ruling class may be just as truly a crowd as the insurrectionary mob, and that the violent behavior of revolutionary crowds is simply the logic of crowd-thinking carried to its swift practical conclusion.

It is generally assumed that a revolution is a sudden and violent change in the form of government. From what has been said it will be seen that this definition is too narrow. History will bear me out in this. The Protestant Reformation was certainly a revolution, as Le Bon has shown, but it affected more than the government or even the organization of the Church. The French Revolu-

tion changed the form of the government in
France several times before it was done, passing through a period of imperial rule and even
a restoration of the monarchy. But the
revolution as such survived. Even though
later a Bourbon or a prince of the House of
Orleans sat on the throne of France, the re-
stored king or his successor was hardly more
than a figurehead. A new class, the Third
Estate, remained in fact master of France.
There had been a change in the ownership of
the land; power through the control of vested
property rested with the group which in 1789
began its revolt under the leadership of Mira-
beau. A new dictatorship had succeeded the
old. And this is what a revolution is—*the
dictatorship of a new crowd*. The Russian
revolutionists now candidly admit this fact in
their use of the phrase "the dictatorship of the
proletariat." Of course it is claimed that
this dictatorship is really the dictatorship of
"all the people." But this is simply the old
fiction with which every dominant crowd disguises seizure of power. Capitalist republic-
anism is also the rule of all the people, and
the pope and the king, deriving their authority from God, are really but "the servants
of all."

As we have seen, the crowd mind as such
wills to dominate. Society is made up of
struggle groups, or organized crowds, each

seeking the opportunity to make its catch-words realities and to establish itself in the position of social control. The social order is always held intact by some particular crowd which happens to be dominant. A revolution occurs when a new crowd pushes the old one out and itself climbs into the saddle. When the new crowd is only another faction within the existing dominant crowd, like one of our established political parties, the succession will be accomplished without resort to violence, since both elements of the ruling crowd recognize the rules of the game. It will also not result in far-reaching social changes for the same reason. A true revolution occurs when the difference between the dominant crowd and the one which supplants it is so great as to produce a general social upheaval. The Reformation, the French Revolution, and the "Bolshevist" *coup d'etat* in Russia, all were of this nature. A new social leadership was established and secured by a change in each case in the personnel of the ownership of such property as would give the owners the desired control. In the first case there was a transfer of property in the church estates, either to the local congregations, or the state, or the denomination. In the second case the property transferred was property in land, and with the Russian revolutionists landed property was given to the peasants and vested capital turned over to the control of industrial workers.

Those who lay all emphasis on this transfer of property naturally see only economic causes in revolutionary movements. Economics, however, is not a science of impersonal things. It treats rather of men's relations to things, and hence to one another. It has to do with valuations and principles of exchange and ownership, all of which need psychological restatement. The transfer of the ownership of property in times of revolution to a new class is not an end, it is a means to a new crowd's social dominance. The doctrines, ideals, and principles believed by the revolutionary crowd also serve this end of securing its dominance, as do the social changes which it effects, once in power.

Revolutions do not occur directly from abuses of power, for in that case there would be nothing but revolution all the time, since every dominant crowd has abused its power. It is an interesting fact that revolution generally occurs after the abuses of which the revolutionists complain have been in great measure stopped—that is, after the ruling crowd has begun to make efforts at reform. The Reformation occurred in the pontificate of Leo X. If it had been the result of intolerable abuse alone, it would have happened in the time of Alexander VI, Borgia. The French Revolu-

tion fell upon the mild head of Louis XVI,
though the wrongs which it tried to right
mostly happened in the reign of his predecessor. In most cases the abuses, the existence
of which a revolutionary crowd uses for propaganda purposes, are in turn repeated in new
form by itself after it becomes dominant.
The Reformers in the sixteenth and seven-
teenth centuries resorted to much the same
kind of persecution from which they had themselves earlier suffered. The Constituent Assembly, though it had demanded liberty, soon
set up a more outrageous tyranny through its
own committees than any that the Louies
had dreamed of. Bolshevists in capitalist
countries are the greatest advocates of free
speech; in Russia they are the authors of a
very effective press-censorship.

No, it is hardly the abuses which men
suffer from their ruling crowds which cause
insurrection. People have borne the most terrible outrages and suffered in silence for centuries. Russia itself is a good example of this.

*A revolution occurs when the dominant crowd
begins to weaken.* I think we find proof of
this in the psychology of revolutionary propaganda. A general revolution is not made in a
day, each such cataclysm is preceded by a
long period of unrest and propaganda of opposition to the existing order and its beneficiaries.
The Roman Republic began going to pieces

about a hundred years before the battle of
Actium. The social unrest which followed
the Punic Wars and led to the revolt of the
brothers Gracchi was never wholly checked
during the century which followed. The
dominant party had scarcely rid itself of these
troublesome "demagogues" than revolt broke
out among the slave population of Sicily.
This was followed by the revolt of the Italian
peasants, then again by the insurrection of
Spartacus, and this in turn by the civil war
between Marius and Sulla, the conspiracy of
Catiline, the brief triumph of Julius Cæsar
over the Senate, the revenge of the latter in
the assassination of Cæsar, and the years of
turmoil during the Second Triumvirate.

It is doubtful if there was at any time a
very clear or widespread consciousness of the
issues which successively arose during that
unhappy century. It would seem that first
one counter-crowd and then another, representing various elements of the populace, tried
issue with the ruling crowd. The one factor
which remained constant through all this was
the progressive disintegration of the dominant
party. The supremacy of the *Patres Con-
scripti et Equites* became in fact a social
anachronism the day that Tiberius Gracchus
demanded the expropriation of the landed
aristocracy. The ideas whereby the dominant
crowd sought to justify its pre-emptions began

to lose their functional value. Only the un-
disguised use of brute force was left. Such
ideas ceased to convince. Men of unusual
independence of mind, or men with ambitious
motives, who had grown up within the dominant crowd, began to throw off the spell of its
control-ideas, and, by leaving it, to weaken it
further from within. No sooner was this
weakness detected by other groups than every
sort of grievance and partisan interest became a moral justification for efforts to sup-
plant the rulers. The attempt of the dominant crowd to retain its hold by repeating
its traditional justification-platitudes, un-
changed, but with greater emphasis, may
be seen in the orations of Cicero. It would be
well if some one besides high-school students
and their Latin teachers were to take up the
study of Cicero; the social and psychological situation which this orator and writer
of moral essays reveals has some suggestive
similarities to things which are happening
to-day.

The century and more of unrest which preceded both the Reformation and the French
Revolution is in each instance a long story.
But in both there is the same gradual loss of
prestige on the part of the dominant crowd;
the same inability of this crowd to change
with the changes of time; to find new sanctions for itself when the old ones were no

longer believed; the same unadaptability, the same intellectual and moral bankruptcy, therefore, the same gradual disintegration from within; the same resort to sentimentalism and ineffective use of force, the same circle of hungry counter-crowds waiting around with their tongues hanging out, ready to pounce upon that before which they had previously groveled, and to justify their ravenousness as devotion to principle; the same growing fearlessness, beginning as perfectly loyal desire to reform certain abuses incidental to the existing order, and advancing, with every sign of disillusionment or weakness, to moral indignation, open attack upon fundamental control ideas, bitter hostility, augmented by the repressive measures taken by the dominant crowd to conserve a *status quo* which no longer gained assent in the minds of a growing counter-crowd; finally force, and a new dominant crowd more successful now in justifying old tyrannies by principles not yet successfully challenged.

In the light of these historical analogies the record of events during the last seventy-five years in western Europe and America is rather discomforting reading, and I fear the student of social psychology will find little to reassure him in the pitiable lack of intellectual leadership, the tendency to muddle through, the unteachableness and general want of statesmanlike vision displayed by our present dominant crowds. If a considerable number of people of all classes, those who desire change as well as those who oppose it, could free their thinking from the mechanisms of the crowd-mind, it might be possible to find the working solution of some of our pressing social problems and save our communities from the dreadful experience of another revolution. Our hope lies in the socially minded person who is sufficiently in touch with reality to be also a non-crowd man.

Anyone who is acquainted with the state of the public mind at present, knows that *a priori* arguments against revolution as such are not convincing, except to those who are already convinced on other ground. The dominant crowd in each historical epoch gained its original supremacy by means of revolution. One can hardly make effective use of the commonplace antirevolutionary propaganda of defense of a certain order which has among its most ardent supporters people who are proud to call themselves sons and daughters of the Revolution. Skeptics at once raise the question whether, according to such abstract social ethics, revolutionists become respectable only after they are successful or have been a long time dead. In fact, the tendency to resort to such reasoning is one among many symptoms that the conservative mind has permitted itself to become quite as much a crowd-phenomenon as has the radical mind.

The correct approach here is psychological and pragmatic. There is an increasingly critical social situation, demanding far-reaching reconstructive change; only the most hopeless crowd-man would presume to deny this fact. The future all depends upon the mental processes with which we attempt to meet this situation. Nothing but useless misery can result from dividing crowd against crowd. Crowd-thinking, as I have said, does not solve problems. It only creates ideal compensations and defense devices for our inner conflicts. Conservative crowd-behavior has always done quite as much as anything else to precipitate a revolutionary outbreak. Radical crowd-behavior does not resolve the situation, it only inverts it. Any real solution lies wholly outside present crowd-dilemmas. What the social situation demands most is a different kind of thinking, a new education, an increasing number of people who understand themselves and are intellectually and morally independent of the tyranny of crowd-ideas.

From what has been said above, it follows that revolutionary propaganda is not directly the cause of insurrection. Such propaganda is itself an effect of the unconscious reaction between a waning and a crescent crowd. It is a symptom of the fact that a large number of people have ceased to believe in or assent to the continued dominance of the present controlling crowd and are looking to another.

There is always a tendency among conservative crowds to hasten their own downfall by the manner in which they deal with revolutionary propaganda. The seriousness of the new issue is denied; the crowd seeks to draw attention back to the old issue which it fought and won years ago in the hour of its ascendancy. The fact that the old charms and shibboleths no longer work, that they do not now apply, that the growing counter-crowd is able to psychoanalyze them, discover the hidden motives which they disguise, and laugh at them, is stoutly denied. The fiction is maintained to the effect that present unrest is wholly uncalled-for, that everything is all right, that the agitators who "make people discontented" are alien and foreign and need only be silenced with a time-worn phrase, or, that failing, shut up by force or deported, and all will be well.

I do not doubt that before the Reformation and the French Revolution there were ecclesiastics and nobles aplenty who were quite sure that the masses would never have known they were miserable if meddling disturbers had not taken the trouble to tell them so.

Even an honest critical understanding of the demands of the opposing crowd is discouraged, possibly because it is rightly felt that the critical habit of mind is as destructive of one crowd-complex as the other and the old crowd prefers to remain intact and die in the last ditch rather than risk dissolution, even with the promise of averting a revolution. Hence the Romans were willing to believe that the Christians worshiped the head of an ass. The mediæval Catholics, even at Leo's court, failed to grasp the meaning of the outbreak in north Germany. Thousands saw in the Reformation only the alleged fact that the monk Luther wanted to marry a wife. To-day, one looks almost in vain among business men, editors, and politicians for a more intelligent understanding of socialism. A crowd goes down to its death fighting bogies, and actually running upon the sword of its real enemy, because a crowd, once its constellation of ideas is formed, *never learns anything*.

The crowd-group contains in itself, in the very nature of crowd-thinking, the germs which sooner or later lay it low. When a crowd first becomes dominant, it carries into a place of power a number of heterogeneous elements which have, up to this time, been united in a great counter-crowd because of their common dissatisfaction with the old order. Gradually the special interests of these several groups become separated. The struggle for place is continued as a factional fight within the newly ruling crowd. This factional struggle greatly complicates every revolutionary movement. We witness this in the murderously hostile partisan conflicts which broke out in the revolutionary Assemblies in France. It is seen again in the Reformation, which had hardly established itself when the movement was rent by intense sectarian rivalries of all sorts. The same is true of Russia since the fall of the Tsar, and of Mexico ever since the overthrow of the Diaz regime. If these factional struggles go so far as to result in schism—that is, in a conscious repudiation by one or more factions of the revolutionary creed which had formerly united them all, there is disintegration and in all probability a return to the old ruling crowd.

This reaction may also be made possible by a refusal of one faction to recognize the others as integral parts of the newly triumphant crowd. If the new crowd after its victory can hold itself together, the revolution is established. It then becomes the task of the leading faction in the newly dominant crowd to grab the lion's share of the spoils for itself, give the other factions only so much prestige as will keep alive in their minds the belief that they, too, share in the new victory for "humanity" and hold the new social order together, while at the same time justifying its own leadership by the compulsive power of the idea which they all alike believe. This belief, as we have seen, is the *sine qua non* of the continued existence of any crowd. A dominant crowd survives so long as its belief is held uncritically and repeated and acted upon automatically both by the members of the crowd and its victims. When the factions which have been put at a disadvantage by the leading faction renounce the belief, or awake to the fact that they "have been cheated," disintegration begins.

Between the crowd's professed belief and the things which it puts into practice there is a great chasm. Yet the fiction is uniformly maintained that the things done are the correct and faithful application of the great principles to which the crowd is devoted. We saw in our study of crowd-ideas in general that such ideas are not working programs, but are screens which disguise and apparently justify the real unconscious motive of crowd-behavior. The crowd secures its control, first, by proclaiming in the most abstract form certain generally accepted principles, such as freedom, righteousness, brotherly love — as though these universal "truths" were its own invention and exclusive monopoly. Next, certain logical deductions are made from these principles which, when carried to their logical conclusions regardless of fact or the effect produced, make the thing which the crowd really wants and does appear to be a vindication of the first principles. It is these inferences which go to make up the conscious thinking or belief of the crowd. Thus in the revolutionary convention in France all agree to the principles of Liberty, Equality, and Fraternity. Fidelity to these principles would to a non-crowd mean that the believer should not try to dictate to his fellows what they must believe and choose, that he would exercise good will in his dealings with them and show them the same respect which he wished them to have for himself. But the crowd does not understand principles in this manner. Do all agree to the great slogan of the revolution? Well, then, fidelity to Liberty, Equality, and Fraternity demands that the enemies of these principles and the crowd's definition of them be overthrown. The Mountain is the truly faithful party, hence to the guillotine with the Gironde. This chasm between crowd faith and crowd practice is well illustrated in the case of those Southern patriots in America who were ready to fight and die for the rights of man as expressed in the Declaration of Independence, but refused to apply the principle of the inalienable rights of all men to their own black slaves. Or, again in the case of nineteenth-century capitalism, liberty must be given to all alike. Liberty means equal opportunity. Equal opportunity means free competition in business. Free competition exists only where there is an "incentive"; hence the investor must be encouraged and his gains protected by law. Therefore anti-capitalistic doctrines must be suppressed as subversive of our free institutions. Immigrants to whom for a generation we have extended the hospitality of our slums and labor camps, and the opportunity of freely competing with our well-intrenched corporations, must be made to feel their ingratitude if they are so misguided as to conclude, from the fact that hundreds of leading radicals have been made to serve jail sentences, while after thirty years of enforcing the antitrust law not a single person has ever been sent to prison, that possibly this is not a free land.

Or again—one convicts himself of being a crowd-man who shows partiality among crowds—the principle of democracy is generally accepted. Then there should be industrial democracy as well as political"—hence the "Dictatorship of the Proletariat—for the workers are "the people." Parliamentary assemblies elected by all the people do not necessarily represent labor. Organized labor, therefore, though a minority of the whole, should establish "industrial democracy" by force. So, according to Bolshevist crowd-logic, democracy means the rule of a minority by means of force.

Now it is this fictitious, paranoiac, crowd-logic which one must be able to dispel before he can extricate himself from the clutches of his crowd. If he subjects the whole fabric of abstractions to critical analysis, revalues it, puts himself above it, assumes a pragmatic attitude toward whatever truths it contains, dares to test these truths by their results in experience and to use them for desired ends; if, in short, he scrutinizes his own disguised impulses, brings them to consciousness as what they are, and refuses to be deceived as to their real import, even when they appear dressed in such sheep's clothing as absolutes and first principles, he becomes a non-crowd man, a social being in the best sense.

Those, however, who continue to give assent to the crowd's first principles, who still accept its habit of *a priori* reasoning, merely substituting for its accepted deductions others of their own which in turn serve to conceal and justify their own unconscious desires, will turn from the old crowd only to be gobbled up by a new and counter-crowd. Such people have not really changed. They denounce the old crowd on the ground that "it has not lived up to its principles." It is a significant fact that a crowd's rule is generally challenged in the name of the very abstract ideas of which it has long posed as the champion.

For instance, there is liberty. Every crowd demands it when it is seeking power; no crowd permits it when it is in power. A crowd which is struggling for supremacy is really trying to free itself and as many people as possible from the control of another crowd. Naturally, the struggle for power appears to consciousness as a struggle for liberty as such. The controlling crowd is correctly seen to be a tyrant and oppressor. What the opposition crowd does not recognize is its own wish to oppress, hidden under its struggle for power. We have had occasion to note the intolerance of the crowd-mind as such. A revolutionary crowd, with all its lofty idealism about liberty, is commonly just as intolerant as a reactionary crowd. It must be so in order to remain a crowd. Once it is triumphant it may exert its pressure in a different direction, but the pinch is there just the same. Like its predecessor, it must resort to measures of restraint, possibly even a "reign of terror," in order that the new-won "liberty"—which is to say, its own place at the head of the procession—may be preserved. The denial of freedom appears therefore as its triumph, and for a time people are deceived. They think they are free because everyone is talking about liberty.

Eventually some one makes the discovery that people do not become free just by repeating the magic word "liberty." A disappointed faction of the newly emancipated humanity begins to demand its "rights." The crowd hears its own catchwords quoted against itself. It proceeds to prove that freedom exists by denouncing the disturbers and silencing them, if necessary, by force. The once radical crowd has now become reactionary. Its dream of world emancipation is seen to be a hoax. Lovers of freedom now yoke themselves in a new rebel crowd so that oppressed humanity may be liberated from the liberators. Again, the will to power is clothed in the dream symbols of an emancipated society, and so on around and around the circle, until people learn that with crowds freedom is impossible. For men to attain to mastery of themselves is as abhorrent to one crowd as to another. The crowd merely wants freedom to be a crowd—that is, to set up its own tyranny in the place of that which offends the self-feeling of its members.

The social idealism of revolutionary crowds is very significant for our view of the crowd-mind. There are certain forms of revolutionary belief which are repeated again and again with such uniformity that it would seem the unconscious of the race changes very little from age to age. The wish-fancy which

motivates revolutionary activity always appears to consciousness as the dream of an
ideal society, a world set free; the reign of
brotherly love, peace, and justice. The folly
and wickedness of man is to cease. There will
be no more incentive for men to do evil. The
lion and the lamb shall lie down together.
Old extortions and tyrannies are to be left
behind. There is to be a new beginning,
poverty is to be abolished, God's will is to be
done in earth, or men are at last to live according to reason, and the inalienable rights of all
are to be secured; or the co-operative commonwealth is to be established, with no more
profit-seeking and each working gladly for
the good of all. In other words, the mind of
revolutionary crowds is essentially *eschato-
logical*, or Messianic. The crowd always imagines its own social dominance is a millennium.
And this trait is common to revolutionary
crowds in all historical periods.

We have here the psychological explanation
of the Messianic faith which is set forth with
tremendous vividness in Biblical literature.
The revolutionary import of the social teaching of both the Hebrew and Christian religions
is so plain that I do not see how any honest
and well-informed person can even attempt to
deny it. The telling effectiveness with which
this element in religious teaching may be
used by clever radicals to convict the apolo-

gists of the present social order by the words out of their own mouths is evident in much of the socialist propaganda to-day. The tendency of the will to revolt, to express itself in accepted religious symbols, is a thing to be expected if the unconscious plays the important part in crowd-behavior that we have contended that it does.

The eighth-century Hebrew prophet mingles his denunciations of those who join house to house and field to field, who turn aside the way of the meek, and sit in Samaria in the corner of a couch and on the silken cushions of a bed, who have turned justice to wormwood and cast down righteousness to the earth, etc., etc.,—reserving his choicest woes of course for the foreign oppressors of "my people"—with promises of "the day of the Lord" with all that such a day implies, not only of triumph of the oppressed over their enemies, but of universal happiness.

Similarly the same complex of ideas appears in the writings which deal with the Hebrew "Captivity" in the sixth century B.C., with the revolt of the Maccabeans, and again in the impotent hatred against the Romans about the time of the origin of Christianity.

The New Testament dwells upon some phase of this theme on nearly every page. Blessed are ye poor, and woe unto you who are rich, you who laugh now. The Messiah has come and with him the Kingdom of the Heavens, but at present the kingdom is revealed only to the believing few, who are in the world, but not of it. However, the Lord is soon to return; in fact, this generation shall not pass away until all these things be accomplished. After a period of great trial and suffering there is to be a new world, and a new and holy Jerusalem, coming down from the skies and establishing itself in place of the old. All the wicked, chiefly those who oppress the poor, shall be cast into a lake of fire. There shall be great rejoicing, and weeping and darkness and death shall be no more.

The above sketch of the Messianic hope is so brief as to be hardly more than a caricature, but it will serve to make my point clear, that *Messianism is a revolutionary crowd phenomenon.* This subject has been presented in great detail by religious writers in recent years, so that there is hardly a member of the reading public who is not more or less familiar with the "social gospel." My point is that *all revolutionary propaganda is "social gospel."* Even when revolutionists profess an antireligious creed, as did the Deists of the eighteenth century, and as do many modern socialists with their "materialist interpretation of history," nevertheless the element of irreligion extends only to the superficial trappings of the revolutionary crowd-faith, and even here is not consistent. At bottom the revolutionists' dream of a new world is religious.

I am using the word "religious" in this connection in its popular sense, meaning no more than that the revolutionary crowd rationalizes its dream of a new world-order in imagery which repeats over and over again the essentials of the Biblical "day of the Lord," or "kingdom of heaven" to be established in earth. This notion of cosmic regeneration is very evident in the various "utopian" socialist theories. The Fourierists and St. Simonists of the early part of the nineteenth century were extremely Messianic. So-called "scientific socialists" are now inclined to ridicule such idealistic speculation, but one has only to scratch beneath the surface of present-day socialist propaganda to find under its materialist jargon the same old dream of the ages. A great world-change is to come suddenly. With the triumph of the workers there will be no more poverty or ignorance, no longer any incentive to men to do evil to one another. The famous "Manifesto" is filled with such ideas. Bourgeois society is doomed and about to fall. Forces of social evolution inevitably point to the world-wide supremacy of the working class, under whose mild sway the laborer is to be given the full product of his toil, the exploitation of children is to cease, true liberty will be achieved, prostitution, which is somehow a bourgeois institution, is to be abolished, everyone will be educated, production increased till there is enough for all, the cities shall no more lord it over the rural communities, all alike will perform useful labor, waste places of the earth will become cultivated lands and the fertility of the soil will be increased in accordance with a common plan, the state, an instrument of bourgeois exploitation, will cease to exist; in fact, the whole wicked past is to be left behind, for as

The Communist revolution is the most radical rupture with traditional property relations, no wonder that its development involves the most radical rupture with traditional ideas.

In fine,

In place of the old bourgeois society with its classes and class antagonisms we shall have an association in which the free development of each is the condition for the free development of all.

Le Bon says of the French Revolution:

The principles of the Revolution speedily inspired a wave of mystic enthusiasm analogous to those provoked by the various religious beliefs which had preceded it. All they did was to change the orientation of a mental ancestry which the centuries had solidified.

205

So there is nothing astonishing in the savage zeal of the men of the Convention. Their mystic mentality was the same as that of the Protestants at the time of the Reformation. The principlal heroes of the Terror— Couthon, Saint Just, Robespierre, etc.—were apostles. Like Polyeuctes destroying the altars of the false gods to propagate his faith, they dreamed of converting the globe. . . . The mystic spirit of the leaders of the Revolution was betrayed in the least details of their public life. Robespierre, convinced that he was supported by the Almighty, assured his hearers in a speech that the Supreme Being had "decreed the Republic since the beginning of time."

A recent writer, after showing that the Russian revolution has failed to put the Marxian principles into actual operation, says of Lenin and his associates:

They have caught a formula of glittering words; they have learned the verbal cadences which move the masses to ecstasy; they have learned to paint a vision of heaven that shall outflare in the minds of their followers the shabby realities of a Bolshevik earth. They are master phraseocrats, and in Russia they have reared an empire on phraseocracy.

The alarmists who shriek of Russia would do well to turn their thoughts from Russia's socialistic menace. The peril of Russia is not to our industries, but to our states. The menace of the Bolsheviki is not an economic one, it is a political menace. It is the menace of fanatic armies, drunken with phrases and sweeping forward under Lenin like a Muscovite scourge. It is the menace of intoxicated proletarians, goaded by invented visions to seek to conquer the world.

In Nicolai Lenin the Socialist, we have naught to

fear. In Nicolai Lenin the political chief of Russia's millions, we may well find a menace, for his figure looms over the world. His Bolshevik abracadabra has seduced the workers of every race. His stealthy propaganda has shattered the morale of every army in the world. His dreams are winging to Napoleonic flights, and well he may dream of destiny; for in an age when we bow to phrases, it is Lenin who is the master phraseocrat of the world.

Passing over the question of Lenin's personal ambitions, and whether our own crowd-stupidity, panic, and wrong-headed Allied diplomacy may not have been contributing causes of the menace of Bolshevism, it can hardly be denied that Bolshevism, like all other revolutionary crowd-movements, is swayed by a painted vision of heaven which outflares the miseries of earth. *Every revolutionary crowd of every description is a pilgrimage set out to regain our lost Paradise.*

Now it is this dream of paradise, or ideal society, which deserves analytical study. Why does it always appear the minute a crowd is sufficiently powerful to dream of world-power? It will readily be conceded that this dream has some function in creating certain really desirable social values. But such values cannot be the psychogenesis of the dream. If the dream were ever realized, I think William James was correct in saying that we should find it to be but a "sheep's heaven and lubberland of joy," and that life in it would be so "mawkish and dishwatery" that we should gladly return to this world of struggle and challenge, or anywhere else, if only to escape the deadly inanity.

We have already noted the fact that this dream has the function of justifying the crowd in its revolt and will to rule. But this is by no means all. The social idealism has well been called a dream, for that is just what it is, the daydream of the ages. It is like belief in fairies, or the Cinderella myth. It is the Jack - and - the - beanstalk philosophy. The dream has exactly the same function as the Absolute, and the ideal world-systems of the paranoiac; *it is an imaginary refuge from the real.* Like all other dreams, it is the realization of a wish. I have long been impressed with the static character of this dream; not only is it much the same in all ages, but it is always regarded as the great culmination beyond which the imagination cannot stretch. Even those who hold the evolutionary view of reality and know well that life is continuous change, and that progress cannot be fixed in any passing moment, however sweet, are generally unable to imagine progress going on after the establishment of the ideal society and leaving it behind.

Revolutionary propaganda habitually stops, like the nineteenth-century love story, with a general statement, "and so they lived happily ever after." It is really the end, not the beginning or middle of the story. It is the divine event toward which the whole creation moves, and having reached it, *stops*. Evolution having been wound up to run to just this end, time and change and effort may now be discontinued. There is nothing further to do. In other words, the ideal is lifted clear out of time and all historical connections. As in other dreams, the empirically known sequence of events is ignored. Whole centuries of progress and struggle and piecemeal experience are telescoped into one imaginary symbolic moment. The moment now stands for the whole process, or rather it is *substituted* for the process. We have taken refuge from the real into the ideal. The "Kingdom of Heaven," "Paradise," "The Return to Man in the State of Nature," "Back to Primitive New Testament Christianity," "The Age of Reason," "Utopia," the "Revolution," the "Co-operative Commonwealth," all mean psychologically the same thing. And that thing is not at all a scientific social program, but a symbol of an easier and better world where desires are realized by magic, and everyone's check drawn upon the bank of existence is cashed. *Social idealism of revolutionary crowds is a mechanism of compensation and escape for suppressed desires.*

Is there any easier way of denying the true nature and significance of our objective world than by persuading ourselves that that world is even now doomed, and is bound suddenly to be transformed into the land of our heart's desire? Is it not to be expected that people would soon learn how to give those desires greater unction, and to encourage one another in holding to the fictions by which those desires could find their compensation and escape, by resorting to precisely the crowd-devices which we have been discussing?

The Messianists of Bible times expected the great transformation and world cataclysm to come by means of a divine miracle. Those who are affected by the wave of premillennialism which is now running through certain evangelical Christian communions are experiencing a revival of this faith with much of its primitive terminology.

Evolutionary social revolutionists expect the great day to come as the culmination of a process of economic evolution. This is what is meant by "evolutionary and revolutionary socialism." The wish-fancy is here rationalized as a doctrine of evolution by revolution. Thus the difference between the social revolutionist and the Second Adventist is much smaller than either of them suspects. As Freud would doubtless say, the difference extends only to the "secondary

elaboration of the manifest dream formation"
—the latent dream thought is the same in
both cases. The Adventist expresses the
wish in the terminology of a prescientific age,
while the social revolutionist makes use of
modern scientific jargon. Each alike finds
escape from reality in the contemplation of a
new-world system. The faith of each is a
scheme of redemption—that is, of "compensation." Each contemplates the sudden,
cataclysmic destruction of the "present evil
world," and its replacement by a new order
in which the meek shall inherit the earth.
To both alike the great event is destined, in
the fullness of time, to come as a thief in the
night. In the one case it is to come as the
fulfillment of prophecy; in the other the
promise is underwritten and guaranteed by
impersonal forces of "economic evolution."

This determinism is in the one case what
Bergson calls "radical finalism," and in the
other "radical mechanism." But whether
the universe exists but to reel off a divine
plan conceived before all worlds, or be but
the mechanical swinging of the shuttle of
cause and effect, what difference is there if
the point arrived at is the same? In both
cases this point was fixed before the beginning
of time, and the meaning of the universe is
just that and nothing else, since that is what
it all comes to in the end.

Whether the hand which turns the crank of the world-machine be called that of God or merely "Evolution," it is only a verbal difference; it is in both cases "a power not ourselves which makes for righteousness." And the righteousness? Why, it is just the righteousness of our own crowd—in other words, the crowd's bill of rights painted in the sky by our own wish-fancy, and dancing over our heads like an aurora borealis. It is the history of all crowds that this dazzling pillar of fire in the Arctic night is hailed as the "rosy-fingered dawn" of the Day of the Lord.

Or, to change the figure somewhat, the faithful crowd has but to follow its fiery cloud to the promised land which flows with milk and honey; then march for an appointed time about the walls of the wicked bourgeois Jericho, playing its propaganda tune until the walls fall down by magic and the world is ours. *No revolution is possible without a miracle and a brass band.*

I have no desire to discourage those who have gone to work at the real tasks of social reconstruction—certainly no wish to make this study an apology for the existing social order. In the face of the ugly facts which on every hand stand as indictments of what is called "capitalism," it is doubtful if anyone could defend the present system without recourse to a certain amount of cynicism or cant. The widespread social unrest which has enlisted in its service so much of the intellectual spirit of this generation surely could never have come about without provocation more real than the work of a mere handful of "mischief-making agitators." The challenge to modern society is not wholly of crowd origin.

But it is one thing to face seriously the manifold problems of reconstruction of our social relations, and it is quite another thing to persuade oneself that all these entangled problems have but one imaginary neck which is waiting to be cut with a single stroke of the sword of revolution in the hands of "the people." Hundreds of times I have heard radicals, while discussing certain evils of present society, say, "All these things are but symptoms, effects; to get rid of them you must remove the cause." That cause is always, in substance, the present economic system.

If this argument means that, instead of thinking of the various phases of social behavior as isolated from one another, we should conceive of them as so interrelated as to form something like a more or less causally connected organic whole, I agree. But if it means something else — and it frequently does — the argument is based upon a logical fallacy. The word "system" is not a causal term; it is purely descriptive. The facts referred to, whatever connections we may discover among them, are not the effects of a mysterious "system" behind the facts of human behavior; the facts themselves, taken together, *are* the system.

The confusion of causal and descriptive ideas is a habit common to both the intellectualist philosopher and the crowd-minded. It enables people to turn their gaze from the empirical Many to the fictitious One, from the real to the imaginary. The idea of a system behind, over, outside, and something different from the related facts which the term "system" is properly used to describe, whether that system be a world-system, a logical system, or a social system, whether it be capitalism or socialism, "system" so conceived is a favorite crowd-spook. It is the same logical fallacy as if one spoke of the temperature of this May day as the effect of the climate, when all know that the term climate is simply (to paraphrase James) the term by which we characterize the temperature, weather, etc., which we experience on this and other days. We have already seen to what use the crowd-mind puts all such generalizations.

A popular revolutionary philosophy of history pictures the procession of the ages as made up of a pageant of spook-social systems, each distinct from the others and coming in its appointed time. But social systems do not follow in a row, like elephants in a circus parade—each huge beast with its trunk coiled about the end of his predecessor's tail. The greater part of this "evolutionary and revolutionary" pageantry is simply dream-stuff. Those who try to march into Utopia in such an imaginary parade are not even trying to reconstruct society; they are sociological somnambulists.

The crowd-mind clings to such pageantry because, as we saw in another connection, the crowd desires to believe that evolution guarantees its own future supremacy. It then becomes unnecessary to solve concrete problems. One need only possess an official program of the order of the parade. In other words, the crowd must persuade itself that only one solution of the social problem is possible, and that one inevitable—its own.

Such thinking wholly misconceives the nature of the social problem. Like all the practical dilemmas of life, this problem, assuming it to be in any sense a single problem, is real just because more than one solution is possible. The task here is like that of choosing a career. Whole series of partially foreseen possibilities are contingent upon certain definite choices. Aside from our choosing, many sorts of futures may be equally possible.

Our intervention at this or that definite point is an act by which we will one series of possibilities rather than another into reality. But the act of intervention is never performed once for all. Each intervention leads only to new dilemmas, among which we must again choose and intervene. It is mainly in order to escape from the necessity of facing this terrifying series of unforeseeable dilemmas that the crowd-man walketh in a vain show.

In pointing out the futility of present-day revolutionary crowd-thinking, I am only striving to direct, in however small a degree, our thought and energies into channels which lead toward desired results. It is not by trombones that we are to redeem society, nor is the old order going to tumble down like the walls of Jericho, and a complete new start be given. Civilization cannot be wiped out and begun all over again. It constitutes the environment within which our reconstructive thinking must, by tedious effort, make certain definite modifications. Each such modification is a problem in itself, to be dealt with, not by belief in miracle, but by what Dewey calls "creative intelligence." Each such modification must be achieved by taking all the known facts, which are relevant, into account. As such it is a new adaptation, and the result of a series of such adaptations may be as great and radical a social transformation as one may have the courage to set as the goal of a definite policy of social effort. But there is a world of difference between social thinking of this kind, where faith is a working hypothesis, and that which ignores the concrete problems that must be solved to reach the desired goal, and, after the manner of crowds, dreams of entering fairyland, or of pulling a new world *en bloc* down out of the blue, by the magic of substituting new tyrannies for old.

Revolutionary crowd-thinking is not "creative intelligence." It is *hocus-pocus,* a sort of social magic formula like the "mutabor" in the Arabian Nights; it is an *Aladdin's-lamp* philosophy. And here we may sum up this part of our argument. The idea of the revolution is to the crowd a symbol, the function of which is compensation for the burdens of the struggle for existence, for the feeling of social inferiority, and for desires suppressed by civilization. It is an imaginary escape from hard reality, a new-world system in which the ego seeks refuge, a defense mechanism under the compulsive influence of which crowds behave like somnambulistic individuals. It is the apotheosis of the under crowd itself and the transcendental expression and justification of its will to rule. It is made up of just those broad generalizations which are of use in keeping that crowd together. It gives the new crowd unction in its fight with the old, since it was precisely these same dream-thoughts which the old crowd wrote on its banners in the day when it, too, was blowing trumpets outside the walls of Jericho.

VIII

THE FRUITS OF REVOLUTION—NEW CROWD-TYRANNIES FOR OLD

SO much for the psychology of the revolutionary propaganda. Now let us look at what happens in the moment of revolutionary outbreak. We have dwelt at some length on the fact that a revolution occurs when a new crowd succeeds in displacing an old one in position of social control. At first there is a general feeling of release and of freedom. There is a brief priod of ecstasy, of good will, a strange, almost mystical magnanimity. A flood of oratory is released in praise of the "new day of the people." Everyone is a "comrade." Everyone is important. There is an inclination to trust everyone. This Easter-morning state of mind generally lasts for some days—until people are driven by the pinch of hunger to stop talking and take up again the routine tasks of daily living. We have all read how the "citizens" of the French Revolution danced in the streets for sheer joy in their new-won liberty. Those

who were in Petrograd during the days which
immediately followed the downfall of the Tsar
bear witness to a like almost mystical sense
of the general goodness of human kind and of
joy in human fellowship.

With the return to the commonplace tasks
of daily life, some effort, and indeed further
rationalization, is needed to keep up the
feeling that the new and wonderful age has
really come to stay. Conflicts of interest
and special grievances are viewed as involving
the vital principles of the Revolution. People
become impatient and censorious. There is
a searching of hearts. People watch their
neighbors, especially their rivals, to make
sure that nothing in their behavior shall con-
firm the misgivings which are vaguely felt in
their own minds. The rejoicing and com-
radeship which before were spontaneous are
now demanded. Intolerance toward the van-
quished crowd reappears with increased intensity, not a little augmented by the knowledge that the old enemies are now at "the
people's" mercy.

There is a demand for revenge for old abuses.
The displaced crowd likely as not, foreseeing
the doom which awaits its members, seeks
escape by attempting a counter-revolution.
A propaganda of sympathy is carried on
among members of this same class who remain in the dominant crowd in communities

not affected by the revolution. There is
secret plotting and suspicion of treason on
every hand. People resort to extravagant
expressions of their revolutionary principles,
not only to keep up their own faith in them,
but to show their loyalty to the great cause.
The most fanatical and uncompromising members of the group gain prominence because of
their excessive devotion. By the very logic
of crowd-thinking, leadership passes to men
who are less and less competent to deal with
facts and more and more extreme in their
zeal. Hence the usual decline from the Mira-
beaus to the Dantons and Cariers, and from
these to the Marats and Robespierres, from
the Milukoffs to the Kerenskys and from the
Kerenskys to the Trotzkys. With each excess the crowd must erect some still new
defense against the inevitable disclosure of
the fact that the people are not behaving at
all as if they were living in the kingdom of
heaven. With each farther deviation from
the plain meaning of facts, the revolution
must resort to more severe measures to sustain itself, until finally an unsurmountable
barrier is reached, such as the arrival on the
scene of a Napoleon. Then the majority are
forced to abandon the vain hope of really
attaining Utopia, and content themselves
with fictions to the effect that what they have
really *is* Utopia—or with such other mechan-

isms as will serve to excuse and minimize the significance of existing facts and put off the complete realization of the ideal until some future stage of progress. It is needless to add that those who have most profited by the revolutionary change are also most ready to take the lead in persuading their neighbors to be content with these rational compromises.

Meanwhile, however, the revolutionary leaders have set up a dictatorship of their own, which, while necessary to "save the revolution," is itself a practical negation of the revolutionary dream of a free world. This dictatorship, finally passing into the hands of the more competent element of the revolutionary crowd, justifies itself to the many; professing and requiring of all a verbal assent to the revolutionary creed of which its very existence is a fundamental repudiation. This group becomes in time the nucleus about which society finally settles down again in comparative peace and equilibrium.

In general, then, it may be said that a revolution does not and cannot realize the age-long dream of a world set free. Its results may be summed up as follows: a newly dominant crowd, a new statement of old beliefs, new owners of property in the places of the old, new names for old tyrannies. Looking back over the history of the several great tidal waves of revolution which have swept over the civilization which is to-day ours, it would appear that one effect of them has been to intensify the hold which crowd-thinking has upon all of us, also to widen the range of the things which we submit to the crowd-mind for final judgment. In confirmation of this it is to be noted that it is on the whole those nations which have been burnt over by both the Reformation and the eightenth-century revolution which exhibit the most chauvian brand of nationalism and crowd-patriotism. It is these same nations also which have most highly depersonalized their social relationships, political structures, and ideals. It is these nations also whose councils are most determined by spasms of crowd-propaganda.

The modern man doubtless has a sense of self in a degree unknown—except by the few —in earlier ages, but along with this there exists in "modern ideas," a complete system of crowd-ideas with which the conscious self comes into conflict at every turn. Just how far the revolutionary crowds of the past have operated to provide the stereotyped forms in which present crowd-thinking is carried on, it is almost impossible to learn. But that their influence has been great may be seen by anyone who attempts a psychological study of "public opinion."

Aside from the results mentioned, I think the deposit of revolutionary movements in history has been very small. It may be that, in the general shake-up of such a period, a few vigorous spirits are tossed into a place where their genius has an opportunity which it would otherwise have failed to get. But it would seem that on the whole the idea that revolutions help the progress of the race is a hoax. Where advancement has been achieved in freedom, in intelligence, in ethical values, in art or science, in consideration for humanity, in legislation, it has in each instance been achieved by unique individuals, and has spread chiefly by personal influence, never gaining assent except among those who have power to recreate the new values won in their own experience.

Whenever we take up a new idea as a crowd, we at once turn it into a catchword and a fad. Faddism, instead of being merely a hunger for the new is rather an expression of the crowd-will to uniformity. To be "old-fashioned" and out of date is as truly to be a nonconformist as to be a freak or an originator. Faddism is neither radicalism nor a symptom of progress. It is a mark of the passion for uniformity or *the conservatism of the crowd-mind*. It is change; but its change is insignificant.

It is often said that religious liberty is the fruit of the Reformation. If so it is an indirect result and one which the reformers

224

certainly did not desire. They sought liberty only for their own particular propaganda, a fact which is abundantly proved by Calvin's treatment of Servetus and of the Anabaptists, by Luther's attitude toward the Saxon peasants, by the treatment of Catholics in England, by the whole history of Cromwell's rule, by the persecution of Quakers and all other "heretics" in our American colonies—Pennsylvania, I believe, excepted—down to the date of the American Revolution.

It just happened that Protestantism as *the religion of the bourgeois* fell into the hands of a group, who, outside their religious-crowd interests were destined to be the greatest practical beneficiaries of the advancement of applied science. Between applied science and science as a cultural discipline—that is, science as a humanistic study—the line is hard to draw. The Humanist spirit of the sciences attained a certain freedom, notwithstanding the fact that the whole Reformation was really a reactionary movement against the Renaissance; in spite, moreover, of the patent fact that the Protestant churches still, officially at least, resist the free spirit of scientific culture.

It is to the free spirits of the Italian Renaissance, also to the Jeffersons and Franklins and Paines, the Lincolns and Ingersolls, the Huxleys and Darwins and Spencers, the men who dared alone to resist the religious crowd-mind and to undermine the abstract ideas in which it had intrenched itself, to whom the modern world owes its religious and intellectual liberty.

The same is true of political liberty. England, which is the most free country in the world to-day, never really experienced the revolutionary crowd-movement of the eighteenth century. Instead, the changes came by a process of gradual reconstruction. And it is with just such an opportunist reconstructive process that England promises now to meet and solve the problems of the threatened social revolution. In contrast with Russia, Socialism in England has much ground for hope of success. The radical movement in England is on the whole wisely led by men who with few exceptions can think realistically and pragmatically, and refuse to be swept off their feet by crowd-abstractions. The British Labor party is the least crowd-minded of any of the socialistic organizations of our day. The Rochdale group has demonstrated that if it is co-operation that people desire as a solution of the economic problem, the way to solve it is to co-operate along definite and practicable lines; the co-operators have given up belief in the miracle of Jericho. The British trade-union movement has demonstrated the fact that organization of this kind succeeds in just the degree that it can rise above crowd-thinking and deal with a suggestion of concrete problems according to a statesmanlike policy of concerted action.

To be sure it cannot be denied that the social reconstruction in England is seriously menaced by the tendency to crowd-behavior. At best it reveals hardly more than the superior advantage to the whole community of a slightly less degree of crowd-behavior; but when compared with the Socialist movement in Russia, Germany, and the United States, it would seem that radicalism in England has at least a remote promise of reaching a working solution of the social problem; and that is more than can at present be said for the others.

In the light of what has been said about the psychology of revolution, I think we may hazard an opinion about the vaunted "Dictatorship of the Proletariat"—an idea that has provided some new catchwords for the crowd which is fascinated by the soviet revolution in Russia. Granting for the sake of argument that such a dictatorship would be desirable from any point of view—I do not see how the mere fact that people work proves their capacity to rule, horses also work —would it be possible? I think not. Even the temporary rule of Lenin in Russia can hardly be called a rule of the working class. Bolshevist propaganda will have it that such a dictatorship of the working class is positively necessary if we are ever to get away from the abuses of present "capitalistic society." Moreover, it is argued that this dictatorship of the organized workers could not be undemocratic, for since vested property is to be abolished and everyone forced to work for his living, all will belong to the working class, and therefore the dictatorship of the proletariat is but the dictatorship of all.

In the first place, assuming that it is the dictatorship of all who survive the revolution, this dictatorship of all over each is not liberty for anyone; it may leave not the tiniest corner where one may be permitted to be master of himself. The tyranny of all over each is as different from freedom as is pharisaism from spiritual living.

Again, what is there to show that this imagined dictatorship of all is to be shared equally by all, and if not have we not merely set up a new privileged class—the very thing which the Socialist Talmud has always declared it is the mission of the workers to destroy forever? While the workers are still a counter-crowd, struggling for power against the present ruling class, they are of course held together by a common cause—namely, their opposition to capital. But with labor's triumph, everybody becomes a worker, and there is no one longer to oppose. That which held the various elements of labor together in a common crowd of revolt has now ceased to exist, "class consciousness" has therefore no longer any meaning. Labor itself has ceased to exist *as a class* by reason of its very triumph. What then remains to hold its various elements together in a common cause? Nothing at all. The solidarity of the workers vanishes, when the struggle which gave rise to that solidarity ceases. There remains now nothing but the humanitarian principle of the solidarity of the human race. Solidarity has ceased to be an economic fact, and has become purely "ideological."

Since by hypothesis everyone is a worker, the dictatorship of the workers is a dictatorship based not on labor as such, but upon a universal human quality. It would be quite as truly a dictatorship of everyone if based upon any other common human quality— say, the fact that we are all bipeds, that we all have noses, or the fact of the circulation of the blood. As the purely proletarian character of this dictatorship becomes meaningless, the crowd-struggle switches from that of labor as a whole against capital, to a series of struggles within the dominant labor group itself.

The experience of Russia has even now shown that if the soviets are to save themselves from nation-wide bankruptcy, specially trained men must be found to take charge of their industrial and political activities. Long training is necessary for the successful management of large affairs, and becomes all the more indispensable as industry, education, and political affairs are organized on a large scale. Are specially promising youths to be set apart from early childhood to prepare themselves for these positions of authority? Or shall such places be filled by those vigorous few who have the ambition and the strength to acquire the necessary training while at the same time working at their daily tasks? In either case an *intellectual class* must be developed. Does anyone imagine that this new class of rulers will hesitate to make use of every opportunity to make itself a privileged class?

"But what opportunity can there be," is the reply, "since private capital is to be abolished?" Very well, there have been ruling classes before in history who did not enjoy the privilege of owning private property. The clergy of the Middle Ages was such a class, and their dominance was quite as effective and as enduring as is that of our commercial classes today. But let us not deceive ourselves; in a soviet republic there would be opportunity aplenty for exploitation. As the solidarity of labor vanished, each important trade-group would enter into rivalry with the others for leadership in the co-operative commonwealth. Every economic advantage which any group possessed would be used in order to lord it over the rest.

For instance, let us suppose that the workers in a strategic industry, such as the railways, or coal mines, should make the discovery that by going on a strike they could starve the community as a whole into submission and gain practically anything they might demand. Loyalty to the rest of labor would act no more as a check to such ambitions than does loyalty to humanity in general now. As we have seen, the crowd is always formed for the unconscious purpose of relaxing the social control by mechanisms which mutually justify such antisocial conduct on the part of members of the crowd. There is every reason, both economic and psychological, why the workers in each industry would become organized crowds seeking to gain for their particular groups the lion's share of the spoils of the social revolution. What would there be, then, to prevent the workers of the railroads or some other essential industry from exploiting the community quite as mercilessly as the capitalists are alleged to do at present? Nothing but the rivalry of other crowds who were seeking the same dominance. In time a *modus vivendi* would doubtless be reached whereby social control would be shared by a few of the stronger unions—and their leaders.

The strike has already demonstrated the fact that in the hands of a well-organized body of laborers, especially in those trades where the number of apprentices may be controlled, industrial power becomes a much more effective weapon than it is in the hands of the present capitalistic owners.

A new dictatorship, therefore, must inevitably follow the social revolution, in support of which a favored minority will make use of the industrial power of the community, just as earlier privileged classes used military power and the power of private property. And this new dominance would be just as predatory, and would justify itself, as did the others, by the platitudes of crowd-thinking. The so-called dictatorship turns out, on examination, to be the dictatorship of one section of the proletariat over the rest of it. The dream of social redemption by such means is a pure *crowd-idea*.

IX

FREEDOM AND GOVERNMENT BY CROWDS

THE whole philosophy of politics comes down at last to a question of four words. *Who is to govern?* Compared with this question the problem of the form of government is relatively unimportant. Crowd-men, whatever political faith they profess, behave much the same when they are in power. The particular forms of political organization through which their power is exerted are mere incidentals. There is the same self-laudation, the same tawdry array of abstract principles, the same exploitation of under crowds, the same cunning in keeping up appearances, the same preference of the charlatan for positions of leadership and authority. Machiavelli's Prince, or Dostoievsky's Grand Inquisitor, would serve just as well as the model for the guidance of a Cæsar Borgia, a leader of Tammany Hall, a chairman of the National Committee of a political party, or a Nicolai Lenin.

Ever since the days of Rousseau certain

crowds have persisted in the conviction that all tyrannies were foisted upon an innocent humanity by a designing few. There may have been a few instances in history where such was the case, but tyrannies of that kind have never lasted long. For the most part the tyrant is merely the instrument and official symbol of a dominant crowd. His acts are his crowd's acts, and without his crowd to support him he very soon goes the way of the late Sultan of Turkey. The Cæsars were hardly more than "walking delegates," representing the ancient Roman Soldiers' soviet. They were made and unmade by the army which, though Cæsars might come and Cæsars might go, continued to lord it over the Roman world. While the army was pagan, even the mild Marcus Aurelius followed Nero's example of killing Christians. When finally the army itself became largely Christian, and the fiction that the Christians drank human blood, worshiped the head of an ass, and were sexually promiscuous was no longer good patriotic propaganda, the Emperor Constantine began to see visions of the Cross in the sky. The Pope, who is doubtless the most absolute monarch in the Occident, is, however, "infallible" only when he speaks *ex-cathedra*—that is, as the "Church Herself." His infallibility is that of the Church. All crowds in one way or another claim infallibility. The tyrant Robespierre survived only so long as did his particular revolutionary crowd in France.

The fate of Savonarola was similar. From his pulpit he could rule Florence with absolute power just so long as he told his crowd what it wished to hear, and so long as his crowd was able to keep itself together and remain dominant. The Stuarts, Hohenzollerns, Hapsburgs, and Romanoffs, with all their claims to divine rights, were little more than the living symbols of their respective nation-crowds. They vanished when they ceased to represent successfully the crowd-will.

In general, then, it may be said that *where the crowd is, there is tyranny*. Tyranny may be exercised through one agent or through many, but it nearly always comes from the same source—the crowd. Crowd-rule may exist in a monarchical form of government, or in a republic. The personnel of the dominant crowd will vary with a change in the form of the state, but the spirit will be much the same. Conservative writers are in the habit of assuming that democracy is the rule of crowds pure and simple. Whether crowd-government is more absolute in a democracy than in differently constituted states is a question. The aim of democratic constitutions like our own is to prevent any special crowd from intrenching itself in a position of social control and thus becoming a ruling class. As the experiment has worked out thus far it can hardly be said that it has freed us from the rule of crowds. It has, however, multiplied the number of mutually suspicious crowds, so that no one of them has for long enjoyed a sufficiently great majority to make itself clearly supreme, though it must be admitted that up to the present the business-man crowd has had the best of the deal. The story of the recent Eighteenth Amendment shows how easy it is for a determined crowd, even though in a minority, to force its favorite dogmas upon the whole community. We shall doubtless see a great deal more of this sort of thing in the future than we have in the past. And if the various labor groups should become sufficiently united in a "proletarian" crowd there is nothing to prevent their going to any extreme.

We are passing through a period of socialization. All signs point to the establishment of some sort of social state or industrial commonwealth. No one can foresee the extent to which capital now privately owned is to be transferred to the public. It is doubtful if anything can be done to check this process. The tendency is no sooner blocked along one channel than it begins to seep through another. In itself there need be nothing alarming about this transition. If industry could be better co-ordinated and more wisely administered by non-crowd men for the common good, the change might work out to our national advantage.

It is possible to conceive of a society in which a high degree of social democracy, even communism, might exist along with a maximum of freedom and practical achievement. But we should first have to get over our crowd-ways of thinking and acting. People would have to regard the state as a purely administrative affair. They would have to organize for definite practical ends, and select their leaders and administrators very much as certain corporations now do, strictly on the basis of their competency. Political institutions would have to be made such that they could not be seized by special groups to enhance themselves at the expense of the rest. Partisanship would have to cease. Every effort would have to be made to loosen the social control over the individual's personal habits. The kind of people who have an inner gnawing to regulate their neighbors, the kind who cannot accept the fact of their psychic inferiority and must consequently make crowds by way of compensation, would have to be content to mind their own business. Police power would have to be reduced to the minimum necessary to protect life and keep the industries running.

People would have to become much more capable of self-direction as well as of voluntary co-operation than they are now. They would have to be more resentful of petty official tyranny, more independent in their judgments and at the same time more willing to accept the advice and authority of experts. They would have to place the control of affairs in the hands of the type of man against whose dominance the weaker brethren have in all ages waged war—that is, the free spirits and natural masters of men. All pet dogmas and cult ideas that clashed with practical considerations would have to be swept away.

Such a conception of society is, of course, wholly utopian. It could not possibly be realized by people behaving and thinking as crowds. With our present crowd-making habits, the process of greater socialization of industry means only increased opportunities for crowd-tyranny. In the hands of a dominant crowd an industrial state would be indeed what Herbert Spencer called the "coming slavery."

As it is, the state has become overgrown and bureaucratic. Commissions of all sorts are being multiplied year by year. Public debts are piled up till they approach the point of bankruptcy. Taxes are increasing in the same degree. Statutes are increased in number until one can hardly breathe without

violating some decree, ordinance, or bit of
sumptuary legislation. Every legislative assembly is constantly besieged by the professional lobbyists of a swarm of reformist
crowds. Busybodies of every description
twist the making and the enforcement of law
into conformity with their peculiar prejudices. Censorships of various kinds are growing in number and effrontery. Prohibition is
insincerely put forth as a war measure.
Ignorant societies for the "suppression of
vice" maul over our literature and our art.
Parents of already more children than they
can support may not be permitted lawfully
to possess scientific knowledge of the means of
the prevention of conception. The government, both state and national, takes advantage of the war for freedom to pass again
the hated sort of "alien and sedition" laws
from which the country thought it had freed
itself a century ago. A host of secret agents
and volunteer "guardians of public safety"
are ready to place every citizen under suspicion of disloyalty to the government. Any
advocacy of significant change in established
political practices is regarded as sedition.
An inquisition is set up for the purpose of
inquiring into people's private political opinions. Reputable citizens are, on the flimsiest
hearsay evidence or rumor that they entertain
nonconformist views, subjected to public cen-

sure by notoriety-seeking "investigation commissions"—and by an irresponsible press. Only members of an established political party in good standing are permitted to criticize the acts of the President of the United States. Newspapers and magazines are suppressed and denied the privilege of the mails at the whim of opinionated post-office officers or of ignorant employees of the Department of Justice. An intensely patriotic weekly paper in New York, which happened to hold unconventional views on the subject of religion, has had certain issues of its paper suppressed for the offense of publishing accounts of the alleged misconduct of the Y. M. C. A.

The stupidity and irresponsibility of the Russian spy-system which has grown up in this country along with our overweening state is illustrated by an amusing little experience which happened to myself several months after the signing of the armistice with Germany. All through the trying months of the war the great audience at Cooper Union had followed me with a loyalty and tolerance which was truly wonderful. Though I knew that many had not always been in hearty accord with my rather spontaneous and outspoken Americanism, the Cooper Union Forum was one of the few places in America where foreign and labor elements were present in large numbers in which there was no outbreak or demonstration of any kind which could possibly be interpreted as un-American. We all felt that perhaps the People's Institute with its record of twenty years' work behind it had been of some real service to the nation in adhering strictly to its educational method and keeping its discussions wholly above the level of any sort of crowd-propaganda.

However, in the course of our educational work, it became my task to give to a selected group of advanced students a course of lectures upon the Theory of Knowledge. The course was announced with the title, "How Free Men Think," and the little folder contained the statement that it was to be a study of the Humanist logic, with Professor F. C. S. Schiller's philosophical writings to be used as textbooks. The publication of this folder announcing the course was held up by the printer, and we learned that he had been told not to print it by some official personage whose identity was not revealed. Notwithstanding the fact that Schiller is professor of philosophy in Corpus Christi College, Oxford, and is one of the best-known philosophical writers in the English-speaking world, and holds views practically identical with what is called the "American School," led by the late William James, it developed that the government agents—or whoever they were—objected to the publication of the announcement on the ground that they *thought Schiller was a German*. Such is our intellectual freedom regarding matters which have no political significance whatever, in a world made "safe for democracy." But we must not permit ourselves to despair or grow weary of life in this "safety first" world—waves of pseudo-patriotic panic often follow on the heels of easily won victory. Crowd-phenomena of such intensity are usually of short duration, as these very excesses soon produce the inevitable reaction.

The question, however, arises, is democracy more conducive to freedom than other forms of political organization? To most minds the terms "liberty" and "democracy" are almost synonymous. Those who consider that liberty consists in having a vote, in giving everyone a voice regardless of whether he has anything to say, will have no doubts in the matter. But to those whose thinking means more than the mere repetition of eighteenth-century crowd-ideas, the question will reduce itself to this: Is democracy more conducive to crowd-behavior than other forms of government? Le Bon and those who identify the crowd with the masses would answer with an *a priori* affirmative. I do not believe the question may be answered in any such off-hand manner. It is a question of fact rather than of theory. Theoretically, since we have demonstrated I think that the crowd is not the common people as such, but is a peculiar form of psychic behavior, it would seem that there is no logical necessity for holding that democracy must always and everywhere be the rule of the mob. And we have seen that other forms of society may also suffer from crowd-rule. I suspect that the repugnance which certain aristocratic, and bourgeois writers also, show for democracy is less the horror of crowd-rule as such, than dislike of seeing control pass over to a crowd other than their own. Theoretically at least, democracy calls for a maximum of self-government and personal freedom. The fact that democracy is rapidly degenerating into tyranny of all over each may be due, not to the democratic ideal itself, but the growing tendency to crowd-behavior in modern times. It may be that certain democratic ideals are not so much causes as effects of crowd-thinking and action. It cannot be denied that such ideals come in very handy these days in the way of furnishing crowds with effective catchwords for their propaganda and of providing them with ready-made justifications for their will to power. I should say that democracy has *indirectly permitted*, rather than directly caused, an extension in the range of thought and behavior over which the crowd assumes dictatorship.

In comparing democracy with more auto-
cratic forms of government, this extent or
range of crowd-control over the individual is
important. Of course, human beings will
never permit to one another a very large
degree of personal freedom. It is to the advantage of everyone in the struggle for existence to reduce his neighbors as much as
possible to automatons. In this way one's
own adjustment to the behavior of others is
made easier. If we can induce or compel all
about us to confine their actions to perfect
routine, then we may predict with a fair degree of accuracy their future behavior, and
be prepared in advance to meet it. We all
dread the element of the unexpected, and nowhere so much as in the conduct of our
neighbors. If we could only get rid of the
humanly unexpected, society would be almost
fool - proof. Hence the resistance to new
truths, social change, progress, nonconformity
of any sort; hence our orthodoxies and conventions; hence our incessant preaching to
our neighbors to "be good"; hence the
fanaticism with which every crowd strives to
keep its believers in line. Much of this insistence on regularity is positively necessary.
Without it there could be no social or moral
order at all. It is in fact the source and
security of the accepted values of civilization,
as Schiller has shown.

But the process of keeping one another in line is carried much farther than is necessary to preserve the social order. It is insisted upon to the extent that will guarantee the survival, even the dominance, of the spiritually sick, the morally timid, the trained-animal men, those who would revert to savagery, or stand utterly helpless the moment a new situation demanded that they do some original thinking in the place of performing the few stereotyped tricks which they have acquired; the dog-in-the-manger people, who because they can eat no meat insist that all play the dyspeptic lest the well-fed outdistance them in the race of life or set them an example in following which they get the stomach ache; the people who, because they cannot pass a saloon door without going in and getting drunk, cannot see a moving-picture, or read a modern book, or visit a bathing beach without being tormented with their gnawing promiscuous eroticism, insist upon setting up their own perverted dilemmas as the moral standard for everybody.

Such people exist in great numbers in every society. They are always strong for "brotherly love," for keeping up appearances, for removing temptation from the path of life, for uniform standards of belief and conduct. Each crowd, in its desire to become the majority, to hold the weaker brethren within its fold, and especially as everyone of us has a certain amount of this "little brother" weakness in his own nature, which longs to be pampered if only the pampering can be done without hurting our pride—the crowd invariably plays to this sort of thing and bids for its support. As the little brother always expresses his survival-values in terms of accepted crowd-ideas, no crowd can really turn him down without repudiating its abstract principles. In fact, it is just this weakness in our nature which, as we have seen, leads us to become crowd-men in the first place. Furthermore, we have seen that any assertion of personal independence is resented by the crowd because it weakens the crowd-faith of all.

The measure of freedom granted to men will depend, therefore, upon how many things the crowd attempts to consider its business. There is a law of inertia at work here. In monarchical forms of government, where the crowd-will is exercised through a single human agent, the monarch may be absolute in regard to certain things which are necessary to his own and his crowd's survival. In such matters "he can do no wrong"; there is little or no appeal from his decisions. But the very thoroughness with which he hunts down nonconformity in matters which directly concern his authority, leaves him little energy for other things. Arbitrary power is therefore usually limited to relatively few things, since the autocrat cannot busy himself with everything that is going on. Within the radius of the things which the monarch attempts to regulate he may be an intolerable tyrant, but so long as he is obeyed in these matters, so long as things run on smoothly on the surface, there are all sorts of things which he would prefer not to have brought to his attention, as witness, for instance, the letter of Trajan to the younger Pliny.

With a democracy it is different. While the exercise of authority is never so inexorable—indeed democratic states frequently pass laws for the purpose of placing the community on record "for righteousness," rather than with the intention of enforcing such laws—the number of things which a democracy will presume to regulate is vastly greater than in monarchical states. As sovereignty is universal, everybody becomes lawmaker and regulator of his neighbors. As the lawmaking power is present everywhere, nothing can escape its multieyed scrutiny. All sorts of foibles, sectional interests, group demands, class prejudices become part of the law of the land. A democracy is no respecter of persons and can, under its dogma of equality before the law, admit of no exceptions. The whole body politic is weighed down with all the several bits of legislation which may be demanded by any of the various groups within it. An unusual inducement and opportunity are thus provided for every crowd to force its own crowd-dilemmas upon all.

The majority not only usurps the place of the king, but it tends to subject the whole range of human thought and behavior to its authority—everything, in fact, that anyone, disliking in his neighbors or finding himself tempted to do, may wish to "pass a law against." Every personal habit and private opinion becomes a matter for public concern. Custom no longer regulates; all is rationalized according to the logic of the crowd-mind. Public policy sits on the doorstep of every man's personal conscience. The citizen in us eats up the man. Not the tiniest personal comfort may yet be left us in private enjoyment. All that cannot be translated into propaganda or hold its own in a legislative lobby succumbs. If we are to preserve anything of our personal independence, we must organize ourselves into a crowd like the rest and get out in the streets and set up a public howl. Unless some one pretty soon starts a pro-tobacco crusade and proves to the newspaper-reading public that the use of nicotine by everybody in equal amount is absolutely necessary for the preservation of the American home, for economic efficiency and future military supremacy, we shall doubtless all soon be obliged to sneak down into the cellar and smoke our pipes in the dark.

Here we see the true argument for a written constitution, and also, I think, a psychological principle which helps us to decide what should be in a constitution and what should not. The aim of a constitution is to put a limit to the number of things concerning which a majority-crowd may lord it over the individual. I am aware that the appeal to the Constitution is often abused by predatory interests which skulk behind its phraseology in their defense of special economic privilege. But, nevertheless, people in a democracy may be free only so long as they submit to the dictation of the majority in *just and only those few interests concerning which a monarch, were he in existence, would take advantage of them for his personal ends*. There are certain political and economic relations which cannot be left to the chance exploitation of any individual or group that happens to come along. Some one is sure to come along, for you may be sure that if there is a possible opportunity to take advantage, some one will do it sooner or later.

Now because people have discovered that there is no possible individual freedom in respect to certain definite phases of their common life which are always exposed to seizure by exploiters, democrats have substituted a tyranny of the majority for the tyranny of the one or the favored few which would otherwise be erected at these points. Since it is necessary to give up freedom in these regions anyway, there is some compensation in spreading the tyrannizing around so that each gets a little share of it. But every effort should be made to *limit the tyranny of the majority to just these points*. And the line limiting the number of things that the majority may meddle with must be drawn as hard and fast as possible, since every dominant crowd, as we have seen, will squeeze the life out of everything human it can get its hands on. The minute a majority finds that it can extend its tyranny beyond this strictly constitutionally limited sphere, nothing remains to stop it; it becomes worse than an autocracy. Tyranny is no less abhorrent just because the number of tyrants is increased. A nation composed of a hundred million little tyrants snooping and prying into every corner may be democratic, but, personally, if that ever comes to be the choice I think I should prefer one tyrant. He might occasionally look the other way and leave me a free man, long enough at least for me to light my pipe.

True democrats will be very jealous of government. Necessary as it is, there is no magic about government, no saving grace. Government cannot redeem us from our sins; it will always require all the decency we possess to redeem the government. Government always represents the moral dilemmas of the worst people, not the best. It cannot give us freedom; it can give or grant us nothing but what it first takes from us. It is we who grant to the government certain powers and privileges necessary for its proper functioning. We do not exist for the government; it exists for us. We are not its servants; it is our servant. Government at best is a useful and necessary machine, a mechanism by which we protect ourselves from one another. It has no more rights and dignities of its own than are possessed by any other machine. Its laws should be obeyed, for the same reason that the laws of mechanics should be obeyed—otherwise the machine will not run.

As a matter of fact it is not so much government itself against which the democrat must be on guard, but the various crowds which are always seeking to make use of the machinery of government in order to impose their peculiar tyranny upon all and invade the privacy of everyone. By widening the radius of governmental control, the crowd thus pinches down the individuality of everyone with the same restrictions as are imposed by the crowd upon its own members.

Conway says:

Present-day Democracy rests on a few organized parties. What would a democracy be like if based on millions of independent Joneses each of whom decided to vote this or that way as he pleased? The dominion of the crowd would be at an end, both for better and for worse. We shall not behold any such revolution in the world as we know it. . . .

Thus we must conclude that the crowd by its very nature tends, and always must tend, to diminish (if possible, to the vanishing point) the freedom of its members, and not in one or two respects alone, but in all. The crowd's desire is to swallow up the individuality of its members and reduce them one and all to the condition of crowd units whose whole life is lived according to the crowd-pattern and is sacrificed and devoted to crowd-interests. . . .

An excellent illustration of this crowd-dominance crops up in my afternoon paper. . . . It appears that in certain parts of the country artisans, by drinking too much alcohol, are reducing their capacity of doing their proper work, which happens at the moment to be of great importance to the country at war. Many interferences with liberty are permitted in war time by general consent. It is accordingly proposed to put difficulties in the way of these drinkers by executive orders. One would suppose that the just way to do this would be to make a list of the drinkers and prohibit their indulgence. But this is not the way the crowd works. To it everyone of its constituent members is like another, and all must be drilled and controlled alike. . . . Whatever measure is adopted must fall evenly on all classes, upon club, restaurant and hotel as upon public house. Could anything be more absurd? Lest a gunmaker or a shipbuilder in Glasgow should drink too much, Mr. Asquith must not take a glass of sherry with his lunch at the Athenæum! . . .

GOVERNMENT BY CROWDS

We live in days when crowd dominion over individuals has been advancing at a headlong pace. . . . If he is not to drink in London lest a Glasgow engineer should get drunk, why should not his eating be alike limited? Why not the style and cut of his clothes? Why not the size and character of his house? He must cause his children to be taught at least the minimum of muddled information which the government calls education. He must insure for his dependents the attention of an all-educated physician, and the administration of drugs known to be useless. If the crowd had its way every mother and infant would be under the orders of inspectors, regardless of the capacity of the parent. We should all be ordered about in every relation of life from infancy to manhood. . . . Freedom would utterly vanish, and this, not because the crowd can arrange things better than the individual. It cannot. It lacks the individual's brains. The ultimate reason for all this interference is the crowd's desire to swallow up and control the unit. The instinct of all crowds is to dominate, to capture and overwhelm the individual, to make him their slave, to absorb all his life for their service.

The criticism has often been made of democracy that it permits too much freedom; the reverse of this is nearer the truth. It was de Tocqueville, I think, who first called attention to the "tyranny of the majority" in democratic America. Probably one of the most comprehensive and discriminating studies that have ever been made of the habits and institutions of any nation may be found in the work of this observing young Frenchman who visited our country at the close of its first half century of political independence. De Tocqueville's account of Democracy in America is still good reading, much of it being applicable to the present. This writer was in no sense an unfriendly critic. He praised much that he saw, but even in those days (the period of 1830) he was not taken in by the fiction that, because the American people live under laws of their own making, they are therefore free. Much of the following passages taken here and there from Chapters XIV and XV is as true today as it was when it was written:

America is therefore a free country in which, lest anybody be hurt by your remarks, you are not allowed to speak freely of private individuals, of the State, or the citizens, or the authorities, of public or private undertakings, in short of anything at all, except perhaps the climate and the soil, and even then Americans will be found ready to defend both as if they had concurred in producing them.

The American submits without a murmur to the authority of the pettiest magistrate. This truth prevails even in the trivial details of national life. An American cannot converse—he speaks to you as if he were addressing a meeting. If an American were condemned to confine himself to his own affairs, he would be robbed of one-half of his existence; his wretchedness would be unbearable. . . .

The moral authority of the majority in America is based on the notion that there is more intelligence and wisdom in a number of men united than in a single individual. . . . The theory of equality is thus applied to the intellects of men.

The French, under the old regime, held it for a maxim that the King could do no wrong. The Americans entertain the same opinion with regard to the majority.

In the United States, all parties are willing to recognize the rights of the majority, because they all hope at some time to be able to exercise them to their own advantage. The majority therefore in that country exercises a prodigious actual authority and a power of opinion which is nearly as great (as that of the absolute autocrat). No obstacles exist which can impair or even retard its progress so as to make it heed the complaints of those whom it crushes upon its path. This state of things is harmful in itself and dangerous for the future.

As the majority is the only power which it is important to court, all its projects are taken up with the greatest ardor; but no sooner is its attention distracted than all this ardor ceases.

There is no power on earth so worthy of honor in itself, or clothed with rights so sacred, that I would admit its uncontrolled and all-predominant authority.

In my opinion the main evil of the present democratic institutions of the United States does not arise, as is so often asserted in Europe, from their weakness, but from their irresistible strength. . . . I am not so much alarmed by the excessive liberty which reigns in that country, as by the inadequate securities which one finds against tyranny. When an individual or party is wronged in the United States, to whom can he apply for redress?

It is in the examination of the exercise of thought in the United States that we clearly perceive how far the power of the majority surpasses all the powers with which we are acquainted in Europe. At the present time the most absolute monarchs in Europe cannot prevent certain opinions hostile to their authority from circulating in secret through their dominions and even in their courts.

It is not so in America. So long as the majority is undecided, discussion is carried on, but as soon as its decision is announced everyone is silent. . . .

I know of no country in which there is so little independence of mind and real freedom of discussion as in America. In America the majority raises formidable barriers around the liberty of opinion. Within these barriers an author may write what he pleases, but woe to him if he goes beyond them. Not that he is in danger of an *auto-da-fe*, but he is exposed to continued obloquy and persecution. His political career is closed for ever. Every sort of compensation, even that of celebrity, is refused him. Those who think like him have not the courage to speak out, and abandon him to silence. He yields at length, overcome by the daily effort which he has to make, and subsides into silence as if he felt remorse for having spoken the truth.

Fetters and headsmen were coarse instruments . . . but civilization has perfected despotism itself. Under absolute despotism of one man, the body was attacked to subdue the soul, but the soul escaped the blows and rose superior. Such is not the course adopted in democratic republics; there the body is left free, but the soul is enslaved. . . .

The ruling power in the United States is not to be made game of. The smallest reproach irritates its sensibilities. The slightest joke which has any foundation in truth renders it indignant. Everything must be the subject of encomium. No writer, whatever his eminence, can escape paying his tribute of adoration to his fellow citizens.

The majority lives in the perpetual utterance of

self-applause, and there are certain truths which Americans can only learn from strangers, or from experience. If America has not yet had any great writers, the reason is given in these facts—there can be no literary genius without freedom of opinion, and freedom of opinion does not exist in America.

Such passages as the above, quoted from the words of a friendly student of American democracy, show the impression which, notwithstanding our popular prattle about freedom, thoughtful foreigners have since the beginning received. And de Tocqueville wrote long before crowd-thinking had reached anything like the development we see at present. To-day the tyrannizing is not confined to the majority-crowd. All sorts of minority-crowds, impatient of waiting until they can by fair means persuade the majority to agree with them, begin to practice coercion upon everyone within reach the minute they fall into possession of some slight advantage which may be used as a weapon. From the industrial side we were first menaced by the "invisible government" of organized vested interests; now, by a growing tendency to government by strikes. Organized gangs of all sorts have at last learned the amusing trick of pointing a pistol at the public's head and threatening it with starvation, and up go its hands, and the gang gains whatever it wants for itself, regardless of anyone else. But this "hold-up game" is by no means confined to labor. Capitalistic soviets have since the beginning of the war taken advantage of situations to enhance their special crowd-interests. The following, quoted from a letter written during the war to the *Atlantic Monthly*, by a thoroughly American writer, Charles D. Stewart, describes a type of mob rule which existed in almost every part of the nation while we were fighting for freedom abroad:

Carlyle said that "Of all forms of government, a government of busybodies is the worst." This is true. It is worse than Prussianism, because that is one form of government, at least; and worse than Socialism, because Socialism would be run by law, anyway. But government by busybodies has neither head nor tail; working outside the law, it becomes lawless; and having no law to support it, it finally depends for its enforcement upon hoodlums and mob rule. When the respectable and wealthy elements are resorting to this sort of government, abetted by the newspapers and by all sorts of busybody societies intent upon "government by public sentiment," we finally have a new thing in the world and a most obnoxious one—mob rule by the rich; with the able assistance of the hoodlums—always looking for a chance.

It starts as follows:

The government wishes a certain amount of money. It therefore appeals to local pride; it sets a "quota," which has been apportioned to each locality, and promises of a fine "over-the-top" flag to be hoisted over the courthouse. All well and good; local pride is a very fine thing, competition is wholesome.

But the struggle that ensues is not so much local pride as it looks to be.

Milwaukee, for instance, a big manufacturing center, is noted for its German population. This, the local proprietors fear, may affect its trade. It may be boycotted to some extent. A traveling man comes back and says that a certain dealer in stoves refuses to buy stoves made in Milwaukee!

Ha!—Milwaukee must redeem its reputation; it must always go over the top: it must be able to affix this stamp to all its letters.

Now, as the state has a quota, and the county and city has each its quota, so each individual must have his quota. Each individual must be "assessed" to buy a certain quota [government war loan] of bonds. Success must be made sure: the manufacturers must see the honor of Milwaukee, and Wisconsin, maintained.

It is not compulsory to give a certain "assessed" amount to the Y. M. C. A.; and the government does not make a certain quota of bonds compulsory on citizens—oh, no! it is not compulsory, only you must abide by your assessment. And we will see that you do. No excuse accepted. . . .

Picture to yourself the following "collection committee" traveling out of the highly civilized, "kultured" city of Milwaukee.

Twenty-five automobiles containing sixty to seventy respectable citizens of Milwaukee.

One color guard (a flag at the head) with two home guardsmen in citizens' clothes.

Two deputy sheriffs.

One "official" photographer.

One "official" stenographer.

One banker (this personage to make arrangements to lend a farmer the money in case he protests that he has subscribed too much already).

This phalanx, entirely lawless, moves down upon a farmer who is urging two horses along a cloddy furrow, doing his fall plowing.

They form a semicircle about him; the speechmaker says, "Let us salute the flag" (watching him to see that he does it promptly); and while his horses stand there the speechmaker delivers a speech. He must subscribe his "assessed" amount—no excuses accepted. If he owes for the farm, and has just paid his interest, and has only fifteen dollars to go on with, it makes no difference. He must subscribe the amount of his "assessment," and "sign here."

If not, what happens? The farmer all the time, of course, is probably scared out of his wits, or does not know what to make of this delegation of notables bearing down upon his solitary task in the fields. But if he argues too much, he finds this. They have a large package of yellow placards reading:

THE OCCUPANT OF THESE PREMISES HAS REFUSED TO TAKE HIS JUST SHARE OF LIBERTY BONDS.

And they put them all over his place. He probably signs.

Now bear in mind that this method is not practiced merely against farmers who have made unpatriotic remarks, or have refused to support the war. It is practiced against a farmer who has taken only one hundred dollars when he was assessed a hundred and fifty—and this is to make him "come across" with the remainder.

You might ask, Is this comic opera or is it government?

And now we come to the conclusion. Imagine yourself either a workman in Milwaukee, or a farmer out in the country. You are dealt with in this entirely Prussian manner—possibly the committee, which knows little of your financial difficulties in your home, has just assessed you arbitrarily.

Your constitutional rights do not count. There is no remedy. If you are painted yellow, the District Attorney will pass the buck—he knows what the manufacturer expects of him, and the financier. The state officers of these drives, Federal representatives, are always Milwaukee bankers.

But for you there is no remedy if you are "assessed" too high.

With the Y. M. C. A., and other religious society drives, the same assessment scheme is worked. You cannot give to the Y. M. C. A. You are told right off how much you are to pay.

It would seem that in our democracy freedom consists first of freedom to vote; second, of freedom to make commercial profit; third, of freedom to make propaganda; fourth, of freedom from intellectual and moral responsibility. Each of these "liberties" is little more than a characteristic form of crowd-behavior. The vote, our most highly prized modern right, is nearly always so determined by crowd-thinking that as an exercise of individual choice it is a joke. Men are herded in droves and delivered by counties in almost solid blocks by professional traders of political influence. Before each election a campaign of crowd-making is conducted in which every sort of vulgarity and insincerity has survival value, in which real issues are so lost in partisan propaganda as to become unrecognizable. When the vote is cast it is commonly a choice between professional crowd - leaders whose competency consists in their ability to Billy Sundayize the mob rather than in any marked fitness for the office to which they aspire— also between the horns of a dilemma which wholly misstates the issue involved and is trumped up chiefly for purposes of political advertising. Time and again the franchise thus becomes an agency by which rival crowds may fasten their own tyrannies upon one another.

Freedom to make commercial profit, to get ahead of others in the race for dollars, is what democracy generally means by "opportunity." Nothing is such a give-away of the modern man as the popular use of the word "individualism." It is no longer a philosophy of *becoming* something genuine and unique, but of *getting* something and using it according to your own whims and for personal ends regardless of the effect upon others. This pseudo-individualism encourages the rankest selfishness and exploitation to go hand in hand with the most deadly spiritual conformity and inanity. Such "individualism" is, as I have pointed out, a crowd-idea, for it is motivated by a cheaply disguised ideal of personal superiority through the mere fact of possessing things. Paradoxical as it may appear at first sight, this is really the old crowd notion of "equality," for, great as are the differences of wealth which result, every man may cherish the fiction that he possesses the sort of ability necessary for this kind of social distinction. Such superiority thus has little to do with personal excellence; it is the result of the external accident of success. One man may still be "as good as another."

Against this competitive struggle now there has grown up a counter-crowd ideal of collectivism. But here also the fiction of universal spiritual equality is maintained; the competitive struggle is changed from an individual to a gang struggle, while the notion that personal worth is the result of the environment and may be achieved by anyone whose belly is filled still persists. Proletarians for the most part wish, chinch-bug fashion, to crawl into the Elysian fields now occupied by the hated capitalists. The growing tendency to industrial democracy will probably in the near future cut off this freedom to make money, which has been the chief "liberty" of political democracy until now, but whether liberty in general will be the gainer thereby remains to be seen. One rather prominent Socialist in New York declares that liberty is a "myth." He is correct, in so far as the democratic movement, either political or social, is a crowd-phenomenon. Socialist agitators are always demanding "liberty" nevertheless, but the liberty which they demand is little more than freedom to make their own propaganda. And this leads us to the third liberty permitted by modern democracy.

The "freedom of speech" which is everywhere demanded in the name of democracy is not at all freedom in the expression of individual opinion. It is only the demand for advertising space on the part of various crowds for the publication of their shibboleths and propaganda. Each crowd, while demanding this freedom for itself, seeks to deny it to other crowds, and all unite in denying it to the non-crowd man wherever possible. The Puritan's "right to worship according to the dictates of a man's own conscience" did not apply to Quakers, Deists, or Catholics. When Republicans were "black abolitionists" they would have regarded any attempt to suppress *The Liberator*, as edited by William Lloyd Garrison, as an assault upon the constitutional liberties of the whole nation. But they are not now particularly interested in preserving the constitutional liberties of the nation as represented in the right of circulation of *The Liberator*, edited by Max Eastman. In Jefferson's time, when Democrats were accused of "Jacobinism," they invoked the "spirit of 1776" in opposition to the alien and sedition laws under which their partisan propaganda suffered limitation. To-day, when they are striving to outdo the Republicans in "Americanization propaganda," they actually stand sponsor for an espionage law which would have made Jefferson or Andrew Jackson froth at the mouth. Socialists are convinced that liberty is dead because Berger and Debs are convicted of uttering opinions out of harmony with temporarily dominant crowd-ideas of patriotism. But when Theodore Dreiser was put under the ban for the crime of writing one of the few good novels produced in America, I do not recall that Socialists held any meetings of protest in Madison Square Garden. I have myself struggled in vain for three hours or more on a street corner in Green Point trying to tell liberty-loving Socialists the truth about the Gary schools. When the politicians in our legislative assemblies were tricked into passing the obviously unliberal Eighteenth Amendment, I was much interested in learning how the bulk of the Socialists in the Cooper Union audiences felt about it. As I had expected, they regarded it as an unpardonable infringement of personal freedom, as a typical piece of American Puritan hypocrisy and pharisaism. But they were, on the whole, in favor of it because they thought it would be an aid to Bolshevist propaganda, since it would make the working class still more discontented! Such is liberty in a crowd-governed democracy. . . . It is nothing but the *liberty of crowds to be crowds*.

The fourth liberty in democratic society today is freedom from moral and intellectual responsibility. This is accomplished by the magic of substituting the machinery of the law for self-government, bureaucratic meddlesomeness for conscience, crowd-tyranny for personal decency. Professor Faguet has called democracy the "cult of incompetence" and the "dread of responsibility." He is not far wrong, but these epithets apply not so much to democracy as such as to democracy under the heel of the crowd. The original aim of democracy, so far as its philosophical thinkers conceived of it, was to set genius free from the trammels of tradition, realize a maximum of self-government, and make living something of an adventure. But crowds do not so understand democracy. Every crowd looks upon democracy simply as a scheme whereby it may have its own way. We have seen that the crowd-mind as such is a device for "kidding" ourselves, for representing the easiest path to the enhancement of our self-feeling as something highly moral, for making our personal right appear like universal righteousness, for dressing up our will to lord it over others, as if it were devotion to impersonal principle. As we have seen, the crowd therefore insists

upon universal conformity; goodness means
only making everyone alike. By taking refuge
in the abstract and ready-made system of
crowd-ideas, the unconscious will to power is
made to appear what it is not; the burden of
responsibility is transferred to the group with
its fiction of absolute truth. Le Bon noted the
fact of the irresponsibility of crowds, but
thought that such irresponsibility was due to
the fact that the crowd, being an anonymous
gathering, the individual could lose his identity in the multitude. The psychology of the
unconscious has provided us with what I think
is a better explanation, but the fact of irresponsibility remains and is evident in all the
influence of crowd-thinking upon democratic
institutions. The crowd-ideal of society is one
in which every individual is protected not only
against exploitation, but against temptation—
protected therefore *against himself*. The whole
tendency of democracy in our times is toward
just such inanity. Without the least critical
analysis of accepted moral dilemmas, we are
all to be made moral in spite of ourselves, regardless of our worth, without effort on our
part, moral in the same way that machines
are moral, by reducing the will to mere automatic action, leaving no place for choice and
uncertainty, having everyone wound up and
oiled and regulated to run at the same speed.
Each crowd therefore strives to make its own

moral ideas the law of the land. Law becomes thus a sort of anthology of various existing crowd-hobbies. In the end moral responsibility is passed over to legislatures, commissions, detectives, inspectors, and bureaucrats. Anything that "gets by" the public censor, however rotten, we may wallow in with a perfect feeling of respectability. The right and necessity of choosing our way is superseded by a system of statutory taboos, which as often as not represent the survival values of the meanest little people in the community—the kind who cannot look upon a nude picture without a struggle with their perverted eroticism, or entertain a significant idea without losing their faith.

The effect of all this upon the intellectual progress and the freedom of art in democratic society is obvious, and is just what, to one who understands the mechanisms of the crowd-mind, might be expected. No wonder de Tocqueville said he found less freedom of opinion in America than elsewhere. Explain it as you will, the fact is here staring us in the face. Genius in our democracy is not free. It must beg the permission of little crowd-men for its right to exist. It must stand, hat in hand, at the window of the commissioner of licenses and may gain a permit for only so much of its inspiration as happens to be of use-value to the uninspired. It must play the conformist, pretend to be hydra-headed rather than unique, useful rather than genuine, a servant of the "least of these" rather than their natural master. It must advertise, but it may not prophesy. It may flatter and pat-ronize the stupid, but it may not stand up taller than they. In short, democracy every-where puts out the eyes of its Samson, cuts off his golden-rayed locks, and makes him grind corn to fill the bellies of the Philistines.

From the beginning of the nineteenth cen-tury until now it has been chiefly the business man, the political charlatan, the organizer of trade, the rediscoverer of popular prejudices who have been preferred in our free modern so-cieties. Keats died of a broken heart; Shelley and Wagner were exiled; Beethoven and Schu-bert were left to starve; Darwin was con-demned to hell fire; Huxley was denied his professorship; Schopenhauer was ostracized by the élite; Nietzsche ate his heart out in soli-tude; Walt Whitman had to be fed by a few English admirers, while his poems were pro-hibited as obscene in free America; Emerson was for the greater part of his life *persona non grata* at his own college; Ingersoll was denied the political career which his genius merited; Poe lived and died in poverty; Theodore Parker was consigned to perdition; Percival Lowell and Simon Newcomb lived and died almost unrecognized by the American public.

Nearly every artist and writer and public teacher is made to understand from the beginning that he will be popular in just the degree that he strangles his genius and becomes a vulgar, commonplace, insincere clown.

On the other hand steel manufacturers and railroad kings, whose business record will often scarcely stand the light, are rewarded with fabulous millions and everyone grovels before them. When one turns from the "commercialism," which everywhere seems to be the dominant and most sincere interest in democratic society, when one seeks for spiritual values to counterbalance this weight of materialism, one finds in the prevailing spirit little more than a cult of naïve sentimentality.

It can hardly be denied that if Shakespeare, Boccaccio, Rabelais, Montaigne, Cassanova, Goethe, Dostoievsky, Ibsen, Tolstoi, Rousseau, St. Augustine, Milton, Nietzsche, Swinburne, Rossetti, or even Flaubert, were alive and writing his masterpiece in America today, he would be instantly silenced by some sort of society for the prevention of vice, and held up to the public scorn and ridicule as a destroyer of our innocence and a corrupter of public morals. The guardians of our characters are ceaselessly expurgating the classics lest we come to harm reading them. I often think that the only reason why the Bible is permitted to pass through our mails is because hardly anyone ever reads it.

It is this same habit of crowd-thinking which accounts to a great extent for the dearth of intellectual curiosity in this country. From what we have seen to be the nature of the crowd-mind, it is to be expected that in a democracy in which crowds play an important part the condition described by de Tocqueville will generally prevail. There is much truth in his statement that it seems at first as if the minds of all the Americans "were formed upon the same model." Spiritual variation will be encouraged only in respect to matters in which one crowd differs from another. The conformist spirit will prevail in all. Intellectual leadership will inevitably pass to the "tight-minded." There will be violent conflicts of ideas, but they will be crowd ideas.

The opinions about which people differ are for the most part ready-made. They are concerned with the choice of social mechanisms, but hardly with valuations. With nearly all alike, there is a notion that mankind may be redeemed by the magic of externally manipulating the social environment. There is a wearisome monotony of professions of optimism, idealism, humanitarianism, with little knowledge of what these terms mean.

I am thinking of all those young people who, in the decade and a half which preceded the war, represented the finished product of our colleges and universities. What a stretch of imagination is needed before one may call these young people educated! How little of intellectual interest they have brought back from school to their respective communities! How little cerebral activity they have stirred up! Habits of study, of independent thinking, have seldom been acquired. The "educated" have possibly gained a little in social grace; they have in some cases learned things which are of advantage to them in the struggle for position. Out of the confused mass of un-assimilated information which they dimly re-member as the education which they "got," a sum of knowledge doubtless remains which is greater in extent than that possessed by the average man, but, though greater in extent, this knowledge is seldom different in kind. There is the same superficiality, the same susceptibility to crowd-thinking on every sub-ject. The mental habits of American de-mocracy are probably best reflected to-day by the "best-seller" novel, the *Saturday Evening Post*, the Chautauqua, the Victrola, the moving picture.

Nearly everyone in America can read, for the "schoolhouse is the bulwark of democratic freedom." However, with the decrease in illiteracy there has gone a corresponding low-ering of literary and intellectual standards, a growing timidity in telling the truth, and a passion for the sensationally commonplace. If it be true that before people may be politically free they must be free to function mentally, one wonders how much of an aid to liberty the public schools in this country have been, or if, with their colossal impersonal systems and stereotyped methods of instruction, they have not rather on the whole succeeded chiefly in making learning uninteresting, dulling curiosity and killing habits of independent thinking. There is probably no public institution where the spirit of the crowd reigns to the extent that it does in the public school. The aim seems to be to mold the child to type, make him the good, plodding citizen, teaching him only so much as some one thinks it is to the public's interest that he should know. I am sure that everyone who is familiar with the actions of the school authorities in New York City during the two years, 1918 and 1919, will be impelled to look elsewhere for much of that liberty which is supposed to go with democracy.

Some years ago I conducted a little investigation into the mental habits of the average high-school graduate. An examination was made of twenty or more young people who had been out of school one year. This is doubtless too limited a number to give the findings great general significance, but I give the results in brief for what they are worth. These students had been in school for eleven years. I thought that they ought at least to have a minimum of general cultural information and to be able to express some sort of opinion about the commonplaces of our spiritual heritage. The questions asked were such as follow: What is the difference between the Declaration of Independence and the Constitution of the United States? What is a dicotyledon? Does the name Darwin mean anything to you? Have you ever heard of William James? What is the significance of the battle of Tours? Who was Thomas Jefferson? There were twenty questions in all. The average grade, even with the most liberal marking, was 44.6. The general average was raised by one pupil who made a grade of 69. But then we should not be too severe upon the public-school graduate. One of the brightest college graduates I know left a large Eastern institution believing that Karl Marx was a philologist. Another, a graduate from a Western college, thought that Venus de Milo was an Italian count who had been born without any arms. I know a prominent physician, whose scientific training is such that he has been a lecturer in a medical college, who believes that Heaven is located just a few miles up in the sky, beyond the Milky Way. These are doubtless exceptional cases, but how many

persons with university degrees are there who
have really caught the spirit of the humanistic culture, or have ever stopped to think
why the humanities are taught in our colleges? How many are capable of discriminating criticism of works of music, or painting,
literature, or philosophy? My own experience convinces me, and I am sure that other
public teachers who have had a like experience
will bear witness to the same lamentable fact,
that such little genuine intellectual interest as
there is in this country is chiefly confined to
immigrant Jews, our American youth being,
on the whole, innocent of it. The significance
of this fact is obvious, as is its cause. Due to
the conformist spirit of the dominant crowd,
native-born Americans are losing their intellectual leadership.

We must not ignore the fact that there is
among the educated here a small and, let us
hope, growing group of youthful "intellectuals." But in the first place the proportion of
these to the whole mass is tragically small.
In the second place intellectual liberalism has
been content for the most part to tag along
behind the labor movement, as if the chief
meaning of the intellectual awakening were
economic. It is no disparagement of labor to
say that the intellect in this country of crowds
has also other work to do, and that, until it
strikes out for itself, neither the labor move-

ment nor anything else will rise above commonplace crowd dilemmas. Too much of our so-called intellectualism is merely the substitution of ready-made proletarian crowd-ideas for the traditional crowd-ideas which pass for thinking among the middle classes.

All the facts which have been pointed out above are the inevitable consequences of government by crowds. There can be no real liberty with crowds because there can be no personal independence. The psychic mechanisms of the crowd are hostile to conscious personality. The independent thinker cannot be controlled by catchwords. In our day intellectual freedom is not smothered in actual martyr fires, but it is too often strangled in the cradle. The existence of new values, a thing which will inevitably happen where the human spirit is left free in its creative impulses, is disturbing to the crowd-mind. Education must therefore be made "safe for democracy"; it must be guarded carefully lest the youth become an original personal fact, a new spiritual creation. I realize the element of truth in the statement often made, that there is already too much spiritual originality in the youths of this generation. I am not contending that certain phases of egoism should not be checked by education. A solid intellectual basis must be created which will make social living possible. The trouble is,

however, that this task is done too well. It is
the merely useful man, not the unusual man,
whom the crowd loves. Skill is encouraged,
for, whether it be skill in serving or in demanding service, skill in itself does not upset
existing crowd-values. Reflection is "wicked"
for it leads to doubt, and doubt is non-
gregarious behavior. Education ceases to be
the path of spiritual freedom; it becomes a device for harnessing the spirit of youth in the
treadmill of the survival-values of the crowd.
It is also the revenge of the old against the
young, a way of making them less troublesome. It teaches the rules for success in a
crowd-governed world while taking advantage
of the natural credulity of childhood to draw
the curtain with such terrifying mummery
about the figure of wisdom that the average
mind, never having the daring or curiosity to
lift it, will remain to its dying day a dullard
and a mental slave without suspecting the
fact. Every "dangerous" thought is de-
natured and expurgated. The student is skillfully insulated from any mental shock that
might galvanize him into original intellectual
life. The classic languages are taught for
purposes of "discipline." After six or seven
years' study of Greek literature in the accepted
manner one may be able to repeat most of the
rules of Goodwin's *Greek Grammar*, and pride
himself upon being a cultivated person, know-

ing in the end less of the language than a bootblack from modern Athens knows of it, or than a waiter from Bologna knows of English after one year's residence in Greenwich Village. And the all-important thing is that never once has the student been given a glimpse of the beautiful free pagan life which all this literature is about.

Science is taught that the student, if he has ability, may learn how to make a geological survey of oil lands, construct and operate a cement factory, make poison gas, remove infected tonsils, or grow a culture of bacteria; but should he cease to hold popular beliefs about the origin of life or the immortality of the soul it is well for him to keep the tragic fact to himself. Those who teach history, economics, and political science in such a way as to stimulate independence of thinking on the part of the students are likely to be dismissed from their faculties by the practical business men who constitute the boards of trustees of our institutions of higher learning; the purpose of these sciences is to make our youth more patriotic. Finally, the average instructor receives less pay than a policeman, or a head-waiter, and the unconscious reason for this is all of a piece with the psychology of the crowd-mind. The ignorant man's resentment toward superiority, or "highbrowism," is thereby vindicated. Moreover, the integrity of the complex of ruling crowd-ideas is less endangered. There is less likelihood of its being undermined in the process of education when vigorous, independent spirits are diverted from intellectual pursuits by richer prizes offered in other fields, and the task of instruction therefore left largely to the underfed and timid who are destined by temperament to trot between the shafts.

In this discussion of the government of crowds I have ignored consideration of the mechanisms of political and social organizations which usually characterize the treatment of this subject. It is not that I wish to divert attention from the necessity of more practical and just social arrangements and political forms of organizations. These we must achieve. But the facts which ultimately make for our freedom or slavery are of the mind. The statement that we cannot be politically or economically a free people until we attain mental freedom is a platitude, but it is one which needs special emphasis in this day when all attention is directed to the external form of organization.

No tyranny was ever for long maintained by force. All tyrannies begin and end in the tyranny of ideas uncritically accepted. It is of just such ideas that the conscious thinking of the crowd consists, and it is ultimately from the crowd as a psychological mechanism that tyranny as such proceeds. Democracy in America fails of freedom, not because of our political constitution, though that would doubtless be modified by a people who were more free at heart; it fails because freedom of opinion, intellectual alertness, critical thinking about fundamentals, is not encouraged. There is, moreover, little promise of greater freedom in the various revolutionary crowds who to-day want freedom only to add to the number of crowds which pester us. And for this we have, whether we are radicals or reactionaries or simply indifferent, no one to blame but ourselves and our own crowd-thinking.

X

EDUCATION AS A POSSIBLE CURE FOR CROWD-THINKING

WE have seen that Democracy in and of itself is no more sure a guarantee of liberty than other forms of government. This does not necessarily mean that we have been forced by our psychological study into an argument against the idea of democracy as such. In fact, it cannot be denied that this form of human association may have decided advantages, both practical and spiritual, if we set about in the right way to realize them. It does not follow that, because the franchise is exercised by all, democracy must necessarily be an orgy of mob rule. If, under our modern political arrangements, it has been shown that the crowd presumes to regulate acts and thought processes hitherto considered purely personal matters, it is also true that the dominance of any particular crowd has, in the long run, been rendered less absolute and secure by the more openly expressed hostility of rival crowds. But crowd-behavior has been known in all historic periods. Democracy cannot be said to have caused it. It may be a mere accident of history that the present development of crowd-mindedness has come along with that of democratic institutions. Democracy has indeed given new kinds of crowds their hope of dominance. It has therefore been made into a cult for the self-justification of various modern crowds.

The formula for realizing a more free and humane common life will not be found in any of the proffered cure-alls and propagandas which to-day deafen our ears with their din. Neither are we now in such possession of the best obtainable social order that one would wish to preserve the *status quo* against all change, which would mean, in other words, the survival of the present ruling crowds. Many existing facts belie the platitudes which these crowds speak in their defense, just as they lay bare the hidden meaning of the magic remedies which are proposed by counter-crowds. There is no single formula for social redemption, and the man who has come to himself will refuse to invest his faith in any such thing—which does not mean, however, that he will refuse to consider favorably the practical possibilities of any proposed plan for improving social conditions.

The first and greatest effort must be to *free democracy from crowd-mindedness, by liberating our own thinking*. The way out of this complex of crowd compulsions is the solitary part of self-analysis and intellectual courage. It is the way of Socrates, and Protagoras, of Peter Abelard, and Erasmus, and Montaigne, of Cervantes and Samuel Butler, of Goethe, and Emerson, of Whitman and William James.

Just here I know that certain conservatives will heartily agree with me. "That is it," they will say; "begin with the individual." Yes, but which individual shall we begin with? Most of those who speak thus mean, begin with some other individual. Evangelize the heathen, uplift the poor, Americanize the Bolshevists, do something to some one which will make him like ourselves; in other words, bring him into our crowd. The individual with whom I would begin is myself. Somehow or other if I am to have individuality at all it will be by virtue of being an individual, a single, "separate person." And that is a dangerous and at present a more or less lonely thing to do. But the problem is really one of practical psychology. We must come out of the crowd-self, just as, before the neurotic may be normal, he must get over his neurosis. To do that he must trace his malady back to its source in the unconscious, and learn the meaning of his conscious behavior as it is related to his unconscious desires. Then he must do a difficult thing—he must *accept the fact of himself at its real worth,*

It is much the same with our crowd-mindedness. If psychoanalysis has therapeutic value by the mere fact of revealing to the neurotic the hidden meaning of his neurosis, then it would seem that an analysis of crowd-behavior such as we have tried to make should be of some help in breaking the hold of the crowd upon our spirits, and thus freeing democracy to some extent from quackery.

To see behind the shibboleths and dogmas of crowd-thinking the "cussedness"—that is, the primitive side—of human nature" at work is a great moral gain. At least the "cussedness" cannot deceive us any more. We have won our greatest victory over it when we drag it out into the light. We can at least wrestle with it consciously, and maybe, by directing it to desirable ends, it will cease to be so "cussed," and become a useful servant. No such good can come to us so long as this side of our nature is allowed its way only on condition that it paint its face and we encourage it to talk piously of things which it really does not mean. Disillusionment may be painful both to the neurotic and to the crowd-man, but the gain is worth the shock to our pride. The ego, when better understood, becomes at once more highly personalized because more conscious of itself, and more truly social because better adjusted to the demands of others. It is this socialized and conscious selfhood which is both the aim and the hope of true democracy.

Such analysis may possibly give us the gift to see ourselves as others do not see us, as we have not wished them to see us, and finally enable us to see ourselves and others and to be seen by them as we really are.

We shall be free when we cease pampering ourselves, stop lying to ourselves and to one another, and give up the crowd-mummery in which we indulge because it happens to flatter our hidden weaknesses! In the end we shall only begin to solve the social problem when we can cease together taking refuge from reality in systems made up of general ideas that we should be using as tools in meeting the tasks from which as crowd-men and neurotics people run away; when we discontinue making use of commonly accepted principles and ideals as defense formations for shameful things in which we can indulge ourselves with a clear conscience only by all doing them together.

There must be an increase in the number of unambitious men, men who can rise above vulgar dilemmas and are deaf to crowd propaganda, men capable of philosophical tolerance, critical doubt and inquiry, genuine companionship, and voluntary co-operation in the achievement of common ends, free spirits who can smile in the face of the mob, who know the mob and are not to be taken in by it.

All this sounds much like the old gospel of conviction of sin and repentance; perhaps it is just that. We must think differently, change our minds. Again and again people have tried the wide way and the broad gate, the crowd-road to human happiness, only to find that it led to destruction in a *cul-de-sac*. Now let us try the other road, "the strait and narrow path." The crowd-path leads neither to self-mastery nor social blessedness. People in crowds are not thinking together; they are not thinking at all, save as a paranoiac thinks. They are not working together; they are *only sticking together*. We have leaned on one another till we have all run and fused into a common mass. The democratic crowd to-day, with its sweet optimism, its warm "brotherly love," is a sticky, gooey mass which one can hardly touch and come back to himself clean. By dissolving everything in "one great union" people who cannot climb alone expect to ooze into the co-operative commonwealth or kingdom of heaven. I am sick of this oozing democracy. There must be something crystalline and insoluble left in democratic America. Somewhere there must be people with sharp edges that cut when they are pressed too hard, people who are still solid, who have im-

penetrable depths in them and hard facets
which reflect the sunlight. They are the hope
of democracy, these infusible ones.

To change the figure, may their tribe increase. And this is the business of every educator who is not content to be a faker. What
we need is not only more education, but a
different kind of education. There is more
hope in an illiterate community where people
hate lying than in a high-school educated
nation which reads nothing but trash and is
fed up on advertising, newspapers, popular
fiction, and propaganda.

In the foregoing chapter, reference was
made to our traditional educational systems.
The subject is so closely related to the mental
habits of democracy that it would be difficult
to overemphasize its importance for our study.
Traditional educational methods have more
often given encouragement to crowd-thinking
than to independence of judgment. Thinking
has been divorced from doing. Knowledge,
instead of being regarded as the foresight of
ends to be reached and the conscious direction
of activity toward such ends, has been more
commonly regarded as the copying of isolated
things to be learned. The act of learning has
been treated as if it were the passive reception
of information imposed from without. The
subject to be learned has been sequestered
and set apart from experience as a whole, with

the result that ideas easily come to be regarded as things in themselves. Systems of
thought are built up with little or no sense of
their connection with everyday problems.
Thus our present-day education prepares in
advance both the ready-made logical systems
in which the crowd-mind takes refuge from
the concretely real and the disposition to accept truth second-hand, upon the authority of
another, which in the crowd-man becomes the
spirit of conformity.

Even science, taught in this spirit may be
destructive of intellectual freedom. Professor
Dewey says that while science has done much
to modify men's thoughts, still

It must be admitted that to a considerable extent
the progress thus procured has been only technical;
it has provided more efficient means for satisfying pre-
existent desires rather than modified the quality of
human purposes. There is, for example, no modern
civilization which is the equal of Greek culture in all
respects. Science is still too recent to have been absorbed into imaginative and emotional disposition.
Men move more swiftly and surely to the realization
of their ends, but their ends too largely remain what
they were prior to scientific enlightenment. This fact
places upon education the responsibility of using science
in a way to modify the habitual attitude of imagination
and feeling, not leave it just an extension of our physical
arms and legs. . . .

The problem of an educational use of science is then
to create an intelligence pregnant with belief in the pos-
sibility of the direction of human affairs by itself. The

method of science ingrained through education in habit means emancipation from rule of thumb and from the routine generated by rule of thumb procedure. . . .

That science may be taught as a set of formal and technical exercises is only too true. This happens whenever information about the world is made an end in itself. The failure of such instruction to procure culture is not, however, evidence of the antithesis of natural knowledge to humanistic concern, but evidence of a wrong educational attitude.

The new kind of education, the education which is to liberate the mind, will make much of scientific methods. But let us notice what it is to set a mind free. Mind does not exist in a vacuum, nor in a world of "pure ideas." The free mind is the functioning mind, the mind which is not inhibited in its work by any conflict within itself. Thought is not made free by the mere substitution of naturalistic for theological dogma. It is possible to make a cult of science itself. Crowd-propaganda is often full of pseudoscientific jargon of this sort. Specialization in technical training may produce merely a high-class trained-animal man, of the purely reflex type, who simply performs a prescribed trick which he has learned, whenever an expected motor-cue appears. In the presence of the unexpected such a person may be as helpless as any other animal. It is possible to train circus dogs, horses, and even horned toads, to behave in this same way. Much so-called scientific training in our schools to-day is of this sort. It results not in freedom, but in what Bergson would call the triumph of mechanism over freedom.

Science, to be a means of freedom—that is, science as culture—may not be pursued as pure theorizing apart from practical application. Neither may a calculating utilitarianism gain freedom to us by ignoring, in the application of scientific knowledge to given ends, a consideration of the ends themselves and their value for enriching human experience. It is human interest which gives scientific knowledge any meaning. Science must be taught in the humanist spirit. It may not ignore this quality of human interest which exists in all knowledge. To do so is to cut off our relations with reality. And the result may become a negation of personality similar to that with which the crowd compensates itself for its unconscious ego-mania.

The reference just made to Humanism leads us next to a consideration of the humanities. It has long been the habit of traditional education to oppose to the teaching of science the teaching of the classic languages and the arts, as if there were two irreconcilable principles involved here. Dewey says that

Humanistic studies when set in opposition to study of nature are hampered. They tend to reduce themselves to exclusively literary and linguistic studies, which in turn tend to shrink to "the classics," to languages no longer spoken. . . . It would be hard to find anything in history more ironical than the educational practices which have identified the "humanities" exclusively with a knowledge of Greek and Latin. Greek and Roman art and institutions made such important contributions to our civilization that there should always be the amplest opportunities for making their acquaintance. But to regard them as *par excellence* the humane studies involves a deliberate neglect of the possibilities of the subject-matter which is accessible in education to the masses, and tends to cultivate a narrow snobbery—that of a learned class whose insignia are the accidents of exclusive opportunity. Knowledge is humanistic in quality not because it is *about* human products in the past, but because of what it *does* in liberating human intelligence and human sympathy. Any subject-matter which accomplishes this result is humane and any subject-matter which does not accomplish it is not even educational.

The point is that it is precisely what a correct knowledge of ancient civilization through a study of the classics *does* that our traditional educators most dread. William James once said that the good which came from such study was the ability to "know a good man when we see him." The student would thus become more capable of discriminating appreciation. He would grow to be a judge of values. He would acquire sharp likes and dislikes and thus set up his own standards of judgment. He would become an independent thinker and therefore an enemy of crowds. Scholars of the

Renaissance knew this well, and that is why in their revolt against the crowd-mindedness of their day they made use of the *litteræ humanores* to smash to pieces the whole dogmatic system of the Middle Ages.

With the picture of ancient life before him the student could not help becoming more cosmopolitan in spirit. Here he got a glimpse of a manner of living in which the controlling ideas and fixations of his contemporary crowds were frankly challenged. Here were witnesses to values contrary to those in which his crowd had sought to bring him up in a docile spirit. Inevitably his thinking would wander into what his crowd considered forbidden paths. One cannot begin to know the ancients as they really were without receiving a tremendous intellectual stimulus. After becoming acquainted with the intellectual freedom and courage and love of life which are almost everywhere manifest in the literature of the ancients, something happens to a man. He becomes acquainted with himself as a valuing animal. Few things are better calculated to make free spirits than these very classics, once the student "catches on."

But that is just the trouble; from the Renaissance till now, the crowd-mind, whether interested politically, morally, or religiously; whether Catholic, or Protestant, or merely Rationalist, has done its level best to keep the

student from "catching on." Educational tradition, which is for the most part only sys-
tematized crowd-thinking, has perverted the
classics into instruments for producing spiritual results of the very opposite nature from
the message which these literatures contain.
Latin and Greek are taught for *purposes of
discipline*. The task of learning them has been
made as difficult and as uninteresting as possible, with the idea of forcing the student to
do something he dislikes, of whipping his spirit
into line and rendering him subservient to intellectual authority. Thus, while keeping up
the external appearance of culture, the effect
is to make the whole thing so meaningless and
unpleasant that the student will never have
the interest to try to find out what it is all
about.

I have said that the sciences and classics
should be approached in the "humanistic"
spirit. The humanist method must be extended to the whole subject-matter of education, even to a revaluation of knowing itself.
I should not say *even*, but *primarily*. It is
impossible here to enter into an extended discussion of the humanist theories of knowledge
as contrasted with the traditional or "intellectualist" theories. But since we have seen
that the conscious thinking of the crowd-
mind consists in the main of abstract and
dogmatic logical systems, similar to the

"rationalizations" of the paranoiac, it is important to note the bearing of humanism upon these logical systems wherever they are found.

A number of years ago, while discussing certain phases of this subject with one of the physicians in charge of a large hospital for the insane, the significance of education for healthy mental life was brought out with great emphasis. It was at the time when psychiatrists were just beginning to make use of analytical psychology in the treatment of mental and nervous disorders.

"The trouble with a great many of our patients," said my friend, "is the fact that they have been wrongly educated."

"Do you mean," I said, "that they have not received proper moral instruction?"

"Yes, but by the proper moral instruction I do not mean quite the same thing that most people mean by that. It all depends on the way in which the instruction is given. Many of these patients are the mental slaves of convention. They have been terrified by it; its weight crushes them; when they discover that their own impulses or behavior are in conflict with what they regard as absolute standards, they cannot bear the shock. They do not know how to use morality; they simply condemn themselves; they seek reconciliation by all sorts of crazy ideas which develop into the psychoneurosis. And the only hope there

is of cure for them is re-education. The
physician, when it is not too late, often to do
any good has to become an educator."

The practice of psychoanalysis as a therapeutic method is really hardly anything more
than re-education. The patient must first be
led to face the fact of himself as he really is;
then he must be taught to revalue conventional
ideas in such a way that he can use these
ideas as instruments with which he may adjust
himself in the various relations of life. This
process of education, in a word, is humanistic.
It is pragmatic; the patient is taught that his
thinking is a way of functioning; that ideas
are instruments, ways of acting. He learns
to value these tendencies to act and to find
himself through the mastery of his own
thinking.

Now we have seen that the neurosis is but
one path of escape from this conflict of self
with the imperatives and abstract ideas
through which social control is exercised. The
second way is to deny, unconsciously, the true
meaning of these ideas, and this, as we have
seen, is crowd-thinking. Here, as in the other
case, the education which is needed is that
which acquaints the subject with the functional nature of his own thinking, which directs
his attention to results, which dissolves the
fictions into which the unconscious takes
refuge, by showing that systems of ideas have

no other reality than what they do and no other meaning than the difference which their being true makes in actual experience somewhere.

We have previously noted the connection between the intellectualist philosophies with their closed systems of ideas, their absolutists, and the conscious thinking of crowds. The crowd finds these systems ready-made and merely backs into them and hides itself like a hermit crab in a deserted seashell. It follows that the humanist, however social he may be, cannot be a crowd-man. He, too, will have his ideals, but they are not made-in-advance goods which all must accept; they are good only as they may be made good in real experience, true only when verified in fact. To such a mind there is no unctuousness, by which ideas may be fastened upon others without their assent. Nothing is regarded as so final and settled that the spirit of inquiry should be discouraged from efforts to modify and improve it.

Generalizations, such as justice, truth, liberty, and all other intellectualist- and crowd-abstractions, become to the humanist not transcendental things in themselves, but descriptions of certain qualities of behavior, actual or possible, existing only where they are experienced and in definite situations. He will not be swept into a howling mob by these big words; he will stop to see what particular things are they which in a given instance are to be called just, what particular hypothesis is it which it is sought to verify and thus add to the established body of truth, whose liberty is demanded and what, to be definite, is it proposed that he shall do with the greater opportunity for action? Let the crowd yell itself hoarse, chanting its abstract nouns made out of adjectives, the humanist will know that these are but words and that the realities which they point to, if they have any meaning at all, are what "they are known as."

This humanist doctrine of the concreteness of the real is important. It is a reaffirmation of the reality of human experience. William James, who called himself a "radical empiricist," made much of this point. Experience may not be ruled out for the sake of an *a priori* notion of what this world ought to be. As James used to say, we shall never know what this world really is or is to become until the last man's vote is in and counted. Here, of course, is an emphasis upon the significance of unique personality which no crowd will grant. Crowds will admit personality as an abstract principle, but not as an active will having something of its own to say about the ultimate outcome of things.

Another important point in which humanism corrects crowd-thinking is the fact that it

regards intellect as an instrument of acting,
and not as a mere copyist of realities earthly
or supermundane. Dewey says:

If it be true that the self or subject of experience is
part and parcel of the course of events, it follows that
the self becomes a knower.   It becomes a mind in virtue
of a distinctive way of partaking in the course of events.
The significant distinction is no longer between a knower
and the world, it is between different ways of being in
and of the movement of things; between a physical
way and a purposive way. . . .
As a matter of fact the pragmatic theory of intelligence means that the function of mind is to project
new and more complex ends to free experience from
routine and caprice.   Not the use of thought to accomplish purposes already given either in the mechanism of
the body or in that of the existent state of society, but
the use of intelligence to liberate and liberalize action,
is the pragmatic lesson. . . . Intelligence as intelligence is
inherently forward looking; only by ignoring its primary function does it become a means for an end already
given.   The latter is servile, even when the end is
labeled moral, religious, esthetic.   But action directed
to ends to which the agent has not previously been
attached inevitably carries with it a quickened and
enlarged spirit.   A pragmatic intelligence is a creative
intelligence, not a routine mechanic.

Hence humanism breaks down the conformist spirit of crowds.   From the simplest to the
most complex, ideas are regarded as primarily
motor, or, rather, as guides to our bodily
movements among other things in our environment.   James says that the stream of life

298

which runs in at our eyes and ears is meant to run out at our lips, our feet, and our finger-tips. Bergson says that ideas are like snap-shots of a man running. However closely they are taken together, the movement always oc-curs between them. They cannot, therefore, give us reality, or the movement of life as such, but only cross-sections of it, which serve as guides in directing the conscious activity of life upon matter. According to James again, there are no permanently existing ideas, or impersonal ones; each idea is an individual activity, known only in the thinking, and is always thought *for a purpose.* As all thinking is purposive, and therefore partial, emphasiz-ing just those aspects of things which are use-ful for our present problem, it follows that the sum total of partial views cannot give us the whole of reality or anything like a true copy of it. Existence as a whole cannot be reduced to any logical system. The One and the Abso-lute are therefore meaningless and are only logical fictions, useful, says James, by way of allowing us a sort of temporary irresponsi-bility, or "moral holiday."

From all this follows the humanist view of Truth. Truth is nothing complete and exist-ing in itself independent of human purpose. The word is a noun made out of an adjective, as I have said. An idea becomes true, says James, when it fits into the totality of our experience; truth is what we say about an idea when it works. It must be made true, by ourselves—that is, verified. Truth is therefore of human origin, frankly, man-made. To Schiller it is the same as the good; it is the attainment of satisfactory relations within experience. Or, to quote the famous humanist creed of Protagoras, as Schiller is so fond of doing, "Man is the measure of all things." The meaning of the world is precisely, for all purposes, its meaning for us. Its worth, both logical and moral, is not something given, but just what we through our activity are able to assign to it.

The humanist is thus thrown upon his own responsibility in the midst of concrete realities of which he as a knowing, willing being is one. His task is to make such modifications within his environment, physical and social, as will make his own activity and that of others with him richer and more satisfactory in the future.

The question arises—it is a question commonly put by crowd-minded people and by intellectual philosophers; Plato asks it of the Protagoreans—how, if the individual man is the measure of all things, is there to be any common measure? How any agreement? May not a thing be good and true for one and not for another? How, then, shall there be any getting together without an outside authority and an absolute standard? The answer, as Schiller and James showed, is obvious; life is a matter of adjustment. We each constitute a part of the other's environment. At certain points our desires conflict, our valuations are different, and yet our experience at these points overlaps, as it were. It is to our common advantage to have agreement at these points. Out of our habitual adjustments to one another, a body of mutual understanding and agreement grows up which constitutes the intellectual and moral order of life. But this order, necessary as it is, is still in the making. It is not something given; it is not a copy of something transcendent, impersonal, and final which crowds may write upon their banners and use to gain uniform submission for anything which they may be able to express in terms which are general and abstract. This order of life is purely practical; it exists for us, not we for it, and because we have agreed that certain things shall be right and true, it does not follow that righteousness and truth are fixed and final and must be worshiped as pure ideas in such a way that the mere repetition of these words paralyzes our cerebral hemispheres.

Doubtless one of the greatest aids of the humanist way of thinking in bringing the individual to self-consciousness is the way in which it orients us in the world of present-day events. It inspires one to achieve a working harmony, not a fictitious haven of rest for the mind interested only in its relations to its own ideas. The unity which life demands of us is not that of a perfect rational system. It is rather the unity of a healthy organism all the parts of which can work together.

Cut up as we are into what Emerson called "fragments of men," I think we are particularly susceptible to crowd-thinking because we are so disintegrated. Thought and behavior must always be more or less automatic and compulsory where there is no conscious coordination of the several parts of it. It is partly because we are the heirs of such a patchwork of civilization that few people today are able to think their lives through. There can be little organic unity in the heterogeneous and unrelated aggregation of half-baked information, warring interests, and irreconcilable systems of valuation which are piled together in the modern man's thinking.

Life may not be reduced to a logical unity, but it is an organic whole for each of us, and we do not reach that organic unity by adding mutually exclusive partial views of it together.

Something happens to one who grasps the meaning of humanism; he becomes self-conscious in a new way. His psychic life becomes a fascinating adventure in a real world. He finds that his choices are real events. He is "set intellectually on fire," as one of our educators has correctly defined education. As Jung would doubtless say, he has "extroverted" himself; his libido, which in the crowd seeks to enhance the ego feeling by means of the mechanism which we have described, now is drawn out and attached to the outer world through the intellectual channel. Selfhood is realized in the satisfactoriness of the results which one is able to achieve. in the very fullness of his activity and the richness of his interests.

Such a free spirit needs no crowds to keep up his faith, and he is truly social, for he approaches his social relationships with intelligent discrimination and judgments of worth which are his own. He contributes to the social, not a copy or an imitation, not a childish wish-fancy furtively disguised, but a psychic reality and a new creative energy. It is only in the fellowship of such spirits, whatever political or economic forms their association may take, that we may expect to see the Republic of the Free.

INDEX

INDEX

INDEX

INDEX

Reformation, the, 182, 192, 225.
Reformers, 157, 270.
Reformist crowds, 151.
Regression, 111, 135.
Religion, 201.
—— Messianism and revolution, 204.
Religious convert, 86.
—— crowds, 151.
—— education, 153.
—— symbolism, 66.
Renaissance, 170, 175, 225, 292.
Repression, 34, 45, 63, 64.
Republicans, the, 264.
Responsibility, sense of, 100.
Revenge, 220.
Revival meetings, 76.
    (See also Sunday, William.)
Revolution, chapter vii, 166, 183.
—— as a crowd phenomenon, 180.
—— psychic causes of, 171.
—— small fruits of, 224.
—— violence in, 167.
Revolution, French, 38, 170, 182, 183, 192, 194, 205, 219.
—— Russian, 9, 183, 206.
Revolutionary creed, 222.
—— crowds, 151, 200.
—— propaganda, 181, 188, 189, 208.
Riots, 106.
Robespierre, 206, 235.
Rochdale movement, 226.
Rolland, Mme., 182.
Roman republic, 187.
Romanoffs, the, 235.
Rossetti, 270.
Rousseau, Jean J., 153, 233, 270.
Rumor, 104.
Russia, pogroms in, 107.
—— revolution in, 186.
—— Socialist movement in, 227.
Russian revolution, 9, 53, 183, 206.

Sadism, 39, 65, 111.
Saint Just, 206.
Saint Simonists, 204.
Salem, Massachusetts, 163.
Sans-culottism, 171.
Saturday Evening Post, 272.
Savonarola, 235.
Saxon peasants, 225.
Schiller, F. C. S., 241, 300, 301.
—— *Humanism* (Second edition. The Macmillan Company, London, 1912), 142.
—— *Studies in Humanism* (Second edition. The Macmillan Company, London, 1912), 144–147.
Schopenhauer, 153, 269.
Schubert, 269.
Science, 159, 278.
—— humanist spirit of, 225.
Self-appreciation, 63.
    (See also Egoism.)
—— consciousness, 301.
—— deception of crowds, 54.
—— defense, a motive of crowd hatred, 125.

Self-appreciation, feeling, 170, 223.
—— hood, 303.
—— pity, 101.
Senate of United States, 114.
Servetus, 225.
Sexuality, repressed, 63.
Shakespeare, 270.
Shakespeare's " Julius Cæsar," 130.
Shelley, 269.
Sioux Indians, 156.
Social behavior, 1, 2.
—— environment, 35, 37.
—— idealism, 200.
—— order, how possible, 301.
—— order, the present, 100.
—— psychology, 11.
—— reconstruction, task of, 212.
—— redemption, dream of, 207, 222, 232.
—— redemption, no formula for, 282.
—— thinking, 2.
Socialism in England, 226.
Socialist, 80.
—— movement in Germany, 227.
—— movement in Russia, 227.
—— movement in United States, 227.
—— philosophy, 210.
Socialists, the, 141, 204, 265.
Socialization, present tendencies toward, 236.
Society, as "Thing-in-itself," 2.
Society for the Prevention of Vice, 114.
Socrates, 283.
South, lynchings in, 106.
Southern mobs, 39.
Soviet republic, 9.
—— spirit, 9.
Soviets, 38.
Spargo, John, 124.
—— *The Psychology of Bolshevism* (Harper & Brothers, 1919), 8.
Spencer, Herbert, 16, 226, 238.
—— *Principles of Sociology* (D. Appleton & Co., New York, 1898), 11.
Spingarn, Maj. J. E., 122.
Spirit of 1776, 264.
Spiritual valuation, 271.
State, bureaucratic, 238.
Stewart, Charles D., 258.
Strikes, 232.
Stuarts, the, 235.
Substitution, phenomenon of, 116.
Suggestion, 33.
Sumner, William Graham, 181.
—— *Folkways* (Ginn & Co., New York, 1906), 11, 181, 169.
Sunday, Rev. William, 24, 42, 76, 172.
Superiority, idea of, 174.
Suppressed wish, 40.
Suspicion, 104.
Survival values, 77.
Swinburne, 270.
Symbolic thought, 20.
Symbolism, religious, 66.

Taboo, 117.
Tammany Hall, 233.

311

THE BEHAVIOR OF CROWDS

THE END

clash of conflicting desires & motives 34